December 7, 1941

Luther Elvin Cisco • Marvin John Clapp • Cullen Benjamin Clark • David Clark Jr. • George Francis Clark • John C Robert William Clark Jr. • Robert Eugene Clarke • Donald Clash • Gerald Lee Clayton • Robert Roland Clayton • Hubert Paul Clem Francis Clifford • Ray Emerson Clift • Lloyd Dale Clippard • Edward Blanchard Cloues • Edward Jay Clough • Ballard Burgher Cobb offin • Marshall Herman Coffman • Mitchell Cohn • George Anderson Coke • Charles Warren Cole • David Lester Cole • Francis Eu ng Collier Jr. • Walter Leon Collier • Austin Collins • Billy Murl Collins • James Earl Collins • Thomas W. Collins • Harold Kenneth in • James Leo Conlin • Richard Earl Connelly • Joseph Ucline Conner • John Gaynor Connolly • Keefe Richard Connolly • Homer Milton Conrad Jr. • Robert Frank Conrad • Walter Ralph Conrad • Edward Leroy Conway • Grant Clark Cook Jr. • Joseph William Cook • Clarence Eugene Cooper • Frank Bernard Cooper • Kenneth Erven Cooper • Kenneth James Cooper • Leon John Corbin • Gerard John Corcoran • Ernest Eugene Corey • Robert Livingston Corn • P. W. Cornelius • Russell Dale Corning • Beoin Hume Corzatt • Richard Lee Coster • Harold Kendall Costill • Louis Albert Costin • Leo Paul Cotner • Charles Edwin Cottier • John H. Couhig • Arthur Lee Coulter • William Cowan • Joel Beman Cowden • Gerald Clinton Cox • William Milford Cox • William Coyne Jr. • Harley Wade Craft • James Edwin Craig • John William Craig • John Reeves Crain • Wallace Dewight Crawley • William C. Creech • Alva J. Cremean • Louis Edward Cremeens • Warren Harding Crim • Michael Criscuolo • Wilfred John Criswell • Theodore Wheeler Croft • Howard Don Cromwell • David Lloyd Crossett • Howard Daniel Crow • Samuel Warwick Crowder • Cecil Thomas Crowe • Thomas Ewing Crowley • John E. Cruthirds • William Joseph Curry • William McKnight Curry • Herbert S. Curtis Jr. • Lloyd B. Curtis • Lyle Carl Curtis • Lloyd Henry Cutrer • Harold Bernard Cybulski • Francis Anton Cychosz • Glenn Gerald Cyriack • Stanley Czarnecki • Theophil Czekajski • Otreste Da Torre • Richard Norbert Dahlheimer • John L. Dains • Edward Carlyle Daly • Lloyd Maxton Daniel • Andrew Joseph Danik • Marshall Eugene Darby Jr. • Phillip Zane Darch • Louis H. Dasenbrock • Paul Eugene Daugherty • Ernest J. Davenport • James Watson Davenport Jr. • Allen Arthur Davis • Billy Rex Davis • Edward Hope Davis • Frederick Curtis Davis • John Quitman Davis • Milton Henry Davis • Murle Melvin Davis • Myrle Clarence Davis • Thomas Ray Davis • Virgil Denton Davis • Walter Mindred Davis • James Berkley Dawson • Francis Daniel Day • William John Day • Donald Edwin De Armoun • Vicente De Castro • Frank J. De Polis • Lyle Bernard Dean • John Wesley Deetz • Russell C. Defenbaugh • Leslie Phillip Delles • Frederick Eugene Delong • Leroy Dennis • Eugene B. Denson • Russell Edwin Deritis • Ralph Alva Derrington • James H. Derthick • John James Dewitt • John Buchanan Dial • Francis Edward Dick • Ralph R. Dick • Ernest Boggio Dickens • Richard A. Dickerson • Douglas R. Dieckhoff • Leaman Robert Dill • John George Dine • Robert Joseph Dineen • Richard Henry Dobbins • Milton Paul Dobey Jr. • Kenneth E. Doernenburg • George Walter Doherty • John Albert Doherty • Marshall Leonard Dompier • John Malcolm Donald • Ned Burton Donohue • John Monroe Dority • Carl David Dorr • Stanley Daniel Dosick • William Hugh Dosser • Ralph Mc Clearn Dougherty • Norman W. Douglas • Eugene Victor Downing • Jack A. Downs • Bernard Vincent Doyle • Wand B. Doyle • Herbert Allen Dreesbach • Elmer Edwin Drefahl • Bill Lester Driver • Donald Landford Drum • Stanislaw Frank Drwall • William Duane • Fred John Ducolon • Louis Felix Ducrest • Robert C. Duff Jr. • Guy Dugger • Lee Herwin Duke • Robert Edward Duke • Billie Joe Dukes • Lonnie William Dukes • Jerald Fraser Dullum • Kenneth Leroy Dunaway • Elmer Marvin Dunham • George S. Dunn Jr. • Robert Wesley Dunnam • Arthur Joseph Dupree • Donat George Duquette Jr. • William Teasdale Durham • Russell Durio • Edward Norman Durkee • Thomas Roy Durning Jr. • Clement Edward Durr • Cyril Isaac Dusset • John Duveene • Alvin Albert Dvorak • Tommy Dye • Buford Harvey Dyer • Daniel A. Dyer Jr. • Wallace Eldred Eakes • Emory Lowell Eaton • Walter Charles Ebel • Eugene Keller Eberhardt • Vincent Henry Eberhart • Charles Louie Echols Jr. • Edward Wesley Echols • Henry Clarence Echternkamp • Robert Norris Edling • Clifton Earle Edmonds • David Bell Edmonston • Bruce Roosevelt Edmunds • Harry Lee Edwards • Lyle O. Edwards • Roland Wayne Edwards • William Frederick Eernisse • Leon Egbert • Robert Ross Egnew • Casper Ehlert • Frank Ehrmantraut Jr. • Paul R. Eichelberger • Vernon Jerome Eidsvig • Philip Ward Eldred • Byron G. Elliott • Earl Maurice Ellis • Francis Arnold Ellis Jr. • Richard Everrett Ellis • Wilbur Danner Ellis • Bruce Harry Ellison • Julius Ellsberry • Royal Elwell • Harold C. Elyard • Bill Eugene Embrey • Jack Marvin Emery • John Marvin Emery • Wesley Vernon Emery • Ronald Burdette Endicott • Stanley Gordon Enger • John Charles England • Richard Boyd England • Leland Earl Erbes • Robert Erickson • Robert William Ernest • Robert Charles Erskine • Stanley Joe Erwin • Walton Aluard Erwin • Carl James Estep • Carl Edwen Estes • Forrest Jesse Estes • Leslie Edgar Etchason • Richard Henry Eulberg • David Delton Evans • Evan Frederick Evans • Mickey Edward Evans • Paul Anthony Evans • William Orville Evans • Woodrow Wilson Evans • James Everett • Alfred Adam Ewell • George Eyed • George Leon Faddis • Paul J. Fadon • Malcolm W. Fairchild • Willard E. Fairchild • Alvin E. Fallis • Edgar Arthur Fansler • Ignacio Camacho Farfan • Alfred Jack Farley • John Wilson Farmer • Luther James Farmer • Matilda Kaliko Faufata • Arthur Armond Favreau • Lawrence Herman Fecho • Nicolas San Nicolas Fegurgur • Jack H. Feldman • Paul V. Fellman • Charlton Hanna Ferguson • Marvin Lee Ferguson Jr. • Homer E. Ferris • John Junior Fess • Stuart H. Fiander • Arnold E. Field • Bernard Fields • Reliford Fields • Robert Auswell Fields • Ralph Elmer Fife • George Arthur Filkins • Allen Brady Fincher • Dexter Wilson Fincher • Woodrow Wilson Finley • William Michael Finnegan • Patrick L. Finney • Henry Amis Firth • Leslie Henry Fischer • Delbert Ray Fisher • James Anderson Fisher • Robert Ray Fisher • Charles Porter III Fisk • Simon Fitch • Kent Blake Fitzgerald • Eugene James Fitzsimmons • Francis Charles Flaherty • James Monroe Flanagan • James Lowell Flannery • Robert Joseph Flannery • Donald Eugene Fleetwood • Frank Norman Floege • Jose San Nicolas Flores • Felicismo Florese • Max Edward Flory • Walter Charles Foley • George Everett Fones • George Perry Foote • George Calvin Ford • Jack C. Ford • William Walker Ford • Elmer Lee Foreman • Clarence Melvin Formoe • Alvie Charles Fortenberry • Rodney Shelton Foss • Rowena Kamohaulani Foster • Jack Foth • George Parten Fowler • Daniel Russell Fox • Gilbert Roy Fox • Jack W. Fox • Lee Fox Jr. • Leroy George Frank • John William Frazier • Charles Donald Frederick • Paul B. Free • Thomas Augusta Free • William Thomas Free • John Edmund French • Joy Carol French • Walter R. French • Robert Niven Frizzell • Neil Daniel Frye • Fred Fugate • Kay Ivan Fugate • Robert Wilson Fulton • Frank Francis Funk • Lawrence Henry Funk • Tedd McKinley Furr • Eugene Dash Fuzi • Angelo Michael Gabriele • Roy Arthur Gager • Leo E. A. Gagne • Michael Galajdik • Stanley C. Galaszewski • Russell E. Gallagher • Nickolas Steve Ganas • Melvyn Amour Gandre • George K. Gannam • Samuel Merritt Gantner • Martin Anthony Gara • Claude Ralph Garcia • Jesus Francisco Garcia • Robert Stillman Garcia • Arthur Joseph Gardner • Ernest Russell Gargaro • Raymond Wesley Garlington • Orville Wilmer Garrett • Robert R. Garrett • Eugene Garris • Gerald Ernest Gartin • Thomas Jones Gary • William Frank Gaudette • Joseph L. B. Gaudrault • Ralph Martin Gaultney • Henry Hamilton Gaver Jr. • Philip Robert Gazecki • Kenneth Edward Gebhardt • Paul Heino Gebser • Kenneth Floyd Geer • Marvin Frederick Geise • Leonard Richard Geller •Samuel Henry Gemienhardt Jr. • George Themistocles George • Roscoe Gholston • Billy Edwin Gibson • George Harvey Gibson • George Edward Giesa • Karl Anthony Giesen • Quentin John Gifford • Kenneth Mace Gift • George Gilbert • George H. Gilbert • Tom Gilbert • Thomas Robert Giles • Richard Eugene Gill • Warren Clayton Gillette • Benjamin Edward Gilliard • James Blackburn Ginn • Michael James Giovenazzo • Harold Reuben Givens • James J. Gleason • Arthur Glenn • Angelo Gobbin • Herman August Goetsch • Wiley Coy Goff • Daryl Henry Goggin • Jack Reginald Goldwater • Charles Clay Gomez Jr. • Edward Gomez Jr. •

In Memoriam

Emma Gonsalves • Bibian Bernard Gonzales • Manuel Gonzales • George Merton Gooch • Joseph Good • Leland Good • Robert Henry Gooding • Clifford George Goodwin • Myron Eugene Goodwin • Robert Goodwin • William Arthur Goodwin • Duff Gordon • Peter Charles Gordon Jr. • Paul Gustavus Gosnell • James E. Gossard Jr. • Edward Webb Gosselin • Joseph Adjutor Gosselin • Allen E. W. Goudy • Arthur Gould • Harry Lee Gould • Rupert Clair Gove • Claude Oliver Gowey • Wesley Ernest Graham • Arthur M. Grendpre • Raymond Edward Granger • Lawrence Everett Grant • Albert James Gray • Lawrence Moore Gray • William James Gray Jr. • Glen Hubert Green • John Sherman Greene • Carroll Gale Greenfield • Robert Donald Greenwald • Charles Norman Gregoire • Daniel Thornburg Griffin • Lawrence J. Griffin • Reese Olin Griffin • Thomas Edward Griffith •Robert Alfred Griffiths • Robert Beryle Grissinger • Warren Wilbert Grosnickle • Edgar David Gross • Milton Henry Gross • Roy Arthur Gross • Vernon Neslie Grow • Richard Gunner Grundstrom • Daniel L. Guisinger Jr. • Arthur K. Gullachson • Elwood R. Gummerson • William Ike Gurganus • Jesse Herbert Gurley • William Fred Gusie • James E. Guthrie • Joseph Herman Guttmann • George Hormer Guy • Curtis Junior Haas • Clarence Frederick Haase • Samuel William Haden • Floyd Bates Haffner • Robert Wesley Haines • Hubert Preston Hall • John Rudolph Hall • Ted Hall • Johnnie W. Hallmark • William Ignatius Halloran • Robert Emile Halterman • Harry John Halvorsen • Harold William Ham • Don Edgar Hamel • Clarence James Hamilton • Edwin Carrell Hamilton • William Holman Hamilton • Dale Reuben Hamlin • George Winston Hammerud • J D Hampton • Ted W Hampton Jr. • Walter Lewis Hampton • Eugene Paul Hann • David Darling Hanna • Francis Leon Hannon • Carlyle B. Hansen • Harvey Ralph Hansen • George Hanson • Helmer Ansel Hanson • Edward Joseph Hanzel • Ai Harada • Charles Eugene Hardin • Kenneth William Hargraves • Charles Ward Harker • William D. Harmon • Robert Joseph Harr • Keith Homer Harrington • Charles Houston Harris • Daniel Fletcher Harris • George Ellsworth Harris • Hiram Dennis Harris • James William Harris • Louis Edward Harris Jr. • Noble Burnice Harris • Peter John Harris • Hugh Braddock Harriss • Carlton H. Hartford • Alvin Hartley • Kenneth Jay Hartley • Max June Hartsoe • Lonnie Moss Hartson • Herold Aloysius Harveson • William E. Hasenfuss Jr. • James Thomas Hasl • Ardrey Vernon Hasty • Kisa Hatate • John Thomas Haughey • Edward Stanley Haven Jr. • James Wallace Haverfield • Harvey Linfille Havins • Anthony Hawkins Jr. • Russell Dean Hawkins • Albert Eugene Hayden • John Doran Hayes • Kenneth Merle Hayes • Curtis James Haynes • Alfred Hays • William Henry Hays • Jack Claudius Hazdovac • Frank Bernard Head • Harold Lloyd Head • Robert Wayne Headington • Verrel Roy Heater • Alfred Grant Heath • Francis Colston Heath • Hadley Irvin Heavin • Francis F. Hebel • Robert Lee Hebel • Warren Guy Heckendorn • Jess Laxton Hedger • Paul Henry Hedrick • Leo Shinn Heely • Edward Joseph Heidt • Wesley John Heidt • Gerald Leroy Heim • William Francis Hellstern • Merritt Cameron Helm • Floyd Dee Helton • Thomas Hembree • Gilbert Allen Henderson • William Walter Henderson • Frank Hendricksen • Jimmie Lee Henrichsen • Otis Wellington Henry • William Ed Henson Jr. • Harvey Christopher Herber • George Herbert • Joseph C. Herbert • Paul Edward Herrick • James Junior Herring • Robert Asher Herriott Jr. • Austin Henry Hesler • Darrel Miller Hess • Anthony Joseph Hessdorfer • Robert Arnold Hibbard • Arthur Lee Hickman • Warren Paul Hickok • Elmer Orville Hicks • Ralph Dueard Hicks • Fred Masayoshi Higa • John A. Hildebrand Jr. • Bartley Talor Hill • Clifford Dale Hill • Edwin Joseph Hill • Merle Chester J. Hillman • Fred Albert Hilt • Wilson Woodrow Hilton • Frank Weaver Hindman • Arvel Clay Hines • Jackie Yoneto Hirasaki • Jitsuo Hirasaki • Robert Yoshito Hirasaki • Shirley Kinue Hirasaki • Denis Hubert Hiskett • William Hislop • Albert Joseph Hitrik • Joseph Parker Hittorff Jr. • Frank Samuel Hoag Jr. • Herbert John Hoard • Garris Vada Hodges • Howard David Hodges • Lester John Hoelscher • Joseph Warren Hoffman • Claude Herbert Holland Jr. • Paul Zepp Hollenbach • Paul Elston Holley • Ralph Hollis • George Sanford Hollowell • Kenneth Laurence Holm • Harry Randolph Holmes • Lowell D. Holmes • Robert Kimball Holmes • James William Holzhauer • Walter Holzworth • Henry Vernon Homer • Earl A. Hood • Joseph Earnest Hood • Kamiko Hookano • Harold W. Hope • Edwin Chester Hopkins • Homer David Hopkins • John J. Horan • Vincent M. Horan • Chester George Hord • Melvin Freeland Horn • James Albert Horner • Harvey Howard Horrell • James William Horrocks • William David Horton • John Emmet Hosler • Emery Lyle Houde • Clem Raymond House • John James Housel • Elmo Howard • George F. Howard • Rolan George Howard • Darrell Robert Howe • Leroy Howell • Clarence E. Hoyt • Charles Lewis Hrusecky • Frank A. Hryniewicz • Haywood Hubbard Jr. • Edgar E. Hubner • Alfred William Hudgell • Robert Chilton Hudnall • Charles Eugene Hudson • Ira Duane Hudson • Robert Glenn Huff • Clyde Franklin Huffman • Bernard Thomas Hughes • Edward Rhys Hughes • Lewis Burton Hughes Jr. • Marvin Austin Hughes • James Clynton Hughey • Doyne Conley Huie • Robert L. Hull • Lorentz Emanuel Hultgren • Donald Standly Hultman • Henry J. Humphrey • Robert Fredrick Hunter • Robert Melvin Hunter • Henry Louis Huntington • Willard Hardy Hurd • Wendell Ray Hurley • Ivan Joseph Huval • Leslie Creade Hux • Arthur Albert Huys • William Hughes Hyde • Joseph Claude Iak • Howard Burt Ibbotson • Paul S. Inamine • Richard Fitch Ingalls • Theodore A Ingalls • David Archie Ingraham • George Washington Ingram • Robert Clement Irish • Orville Adalbert Isham • Luther James Isom • Earl Henry Iversen • Norman Kenneth Iversen • Claydon Ignatius C. Iverson • Charles Andrew Ivey Jr. • Robert Seiko Izumi • David Paul Jackson Jr. • David William Jackson • Lowell Bruce Jackson • Robert Woods Jackson • William Clarence Jackson • Willie Jackson • Richard Fredrick Jacobs • Richard William Jacobs • Dave Jacobson • Herbert Barney Jacobson • Challis Rudolph James • John Burditt James • Edwin Earl Jante • Clifford Thurston Janz • George William Jarding • Edwin Charles Jastrzemski • Kenneth Lyle Jayne • Victor Lawrence Jeans • Joseph Jedrysik • Ira W. Jeffrey • Keith Jeffries • Joseph Herbert Jencuis • Robert Henry Dawson Jenkins • Keith Marlow Jensen • Theodore Que Jensen • Jesse Bennett Jenson • Donald D. Jerrison • Paul Frederick Johann • Charles Homer Johannes • Billy James Johnson • Carl Andreas Johnson • Carl Spencer Johnson • David Andrew Johnson Jr. • Donald Walter Johnson • Edmund Russell Johnson • Edward Dale Johnson • Flavous B. M. Johnson • George Edward Johnson • James Rodman Johnson • John Russell Johnson • Joseph Morris Johnson • Melvin Grant Johnson • Olaf A. Johnson • Robert Henry Johnson • Samuel Earle Johnson • Sterling Conrad Johnson • Jim Hal Johnston • Berry Stanley Jolley • Charles Alan Jones • Charles William Jones • Daniel Pugh Jones • Edmon Ethmer Jones • Edward Watkin Jones • Ernest Jones • Floyd Baxter Jones • Fred M. Jones • George Edwin Jones • Harry Cecil Jones • Henry Jones Jr. • Herbert C. Jones • Homer Lloyd Jones • Hugh Junior Jones • Jerry Jones • Leland Jones • Leroy Henry Jones • Quincy Eugene Jones • Rodney Wallace Jones • Thomas Raymond Jones • Warren Allen Jones • Willard Worth Jones • Woodrow Wilson Jones • Julian Bethune Jordan • Wesley Vernie Jordan • Calvin Wilbur Joyce • Theodore K. Joyner • Albert John Judd • William Arthur Juedes • Thomas Valentine Jurashen • John Louis Kaelin • Harold Lee Kagarice • David Kahookele • Robert Oscar Kaiser • Henry Kalinowski • Eric T. Kampmeyer • Albert Utley Kane • Joseph Nicholas Karabon • John Albert Karli • Eugene Louis Katt • Harry Kaufman • Vernon Paul Keaton • Vincent John Kechner • Billy Mack Keen • Arlie Glen Keener • Howard Verne Keffer • Ralph Henry Keil • George Richard Keith • Donald Garrett Keller • Paul Daniel Keller • James Dennis Kelley • Joe Marion Kelley • Robert R. Kelley • Sanford V. Kelley Jr. • Wilbur Leroy Kellogg • Robert Lee Kelly • Warren Joseph Kempf • Leo Thomas Keninger • Donald Lee Keniston • Kenneth Howard Keniston • Kenneth Frank Kennard • William Henry Kennedy • Charles Cecil Kennington • Milton Homer Kennington • Texas Thomas Kent Jr. • William Harrison Kent • Elmer Tom Kerestes • Raymond Joseph Kerrigan • David Leland Kesler • Isaac Campbell Kidd • Ronald William Kiehn • Charles Ermin Kieselbach • Soon Chip Kim • Robert Doyle Kimmey • Tomaso Kimura • Andrew J. Kinder • Andrew King • Gordon Blane King • Leander Cleaveland King • Lewis Meyer King • Marion E. King Jr. • Orvell Vaniel King Jr. • Robert Nicholas King Jr. • Frederick William Kinney • Gilbert Livingston Kinney • Wilbur Albert Kirchhoff •

continued at back

...we here highly resolve that these dead
shall not have died in vain...
REMEMBER DEC. 7th!

Pacific fortress

As tensions increased between the United States and Japan in the 1930s, the Hawaiian island of Oahu gained importance as a key U.S. military base in the Pacific.

Peaceful paradise

Despite its strategic role, most Americans thought of Hawaii as a tropical Eden. Some twenty-two thousand tourists visited the islands annually in the years before the Second World War.

Launching the attack

A flight of Japanese fighter planes heads for Pearl Harbor after launching from the aircraft carrier *Akagi*. High-level bombers and dive bombers crowd the carrier's deck *(bottom right)*, waiting to join the first wave of the attack. *Painting by C. S. Bailey.*

Deadly aim

This photo, taken from a Japanese attack plane, shows bomb and torpedo damage to the U.S. Pacific Fleet moored along Pearl Harbor's Battleship Row.

DECEMBER 7, 1941

PEARL HARBOR

AMERICA'S DARKEST DAY

BY SUSAN WELS

FOREWORD BY SENATOR DANIEL K. INOUYE

INTRODUCTION BY SIR JOHN KEEGAN

TIME LIFE BOOKS

A TEHABI BOOK

TIME LIFE BOOKS

Time-Life Books is a division of Time Life Inc.
Time-Life is a trademark of Time Warner Inc. and affiliated companies.

TIME LIFE INC.
Chairman and Chief Executive Officer: Jim Nelson
President and Chief Operating Officer: Steven Janas
Senior Executive Vice President and Chief Operations Officer: Mary Davis Holt
Senior Vice President and Chief Financial Officer: Christopher Hearing

TIME-LIFE BOOKS
President: Larry Jellen
Senior Vice President, New Markets: Bridget Boel
Vice President, Home and Hearth Markets: Nicholas M. DiMarco
Vice President, Content Development: Jennifer L. Pearce

TIME-LIFE TRADE PUBLISHING
Vice President and Publisher: Neil S. Levin
Senior Sales Director: Richard J. Vreeland
Director, Marketing and Publicity: Inger Forland
Director of Trade Sales: Dana Hobson
Director of Custom Publishing: John Lalor
Director of Rights and Licensing: Olga Vezeris

PEARL HARBOR
Director of New Product Development: Carolyn M. Clark
New Product Development Manager: Lori A. Woehrle
Executive Editor: Robert Somerville
Director of Design: Tina Taylor
Project Editor: Jennie Halfant
Technical Specialist: Monika Lynde
Design Assistant: Jody Billert

School and library distribution by Time-Life Education, P.O. Box 85026, Richmond, Virginia 23285-5026.

Printed in Hong Kong
10 9 8 7 6 5 4 3 2 1

TEHABI BOOKS

Tehabi Books conceived, designed, and produced *Pearl Harbor* and has developed and published many award-winning books that are recognized for their strong literary and visual content. Tehabi works with national and international publishers, corporations, institutions, and nonprofit groups to identify, develop, and implement comprehensive publishing programs. The name *Tehabi* is derived from a Hopi Indian legend and symbolizes the importance of teamwork. Tehabi Books is located in San Diego, California.
www.tehabi.com

President: Chris Capen
Senior Vice President: Tom Lewis
Vice President of Development: Andy Lewis
Director of Sales and Marketing: Tim Connolly
Director of Trade Relations: Marty Remmell
Editorial Director: Nancy Cash
Art Director: Vicky Vaughn
Editor: Garrett Brown
Map Illustrator: Brian Battles
Copy Editor: Lisa Wolff
Proofreader: Marianna Lee
Editorial Consultant: Daniel Martinez, National Park Service, USS *Arizona* Memorial
Academic Reviewers: Akira Iriye, Harvard University, and Robert Cressman, Naval Historical Center

Photography credits appear on page 224.

Library of Congress Cataloging-in-Publication Data

Wels, Susan.
Pearl Harbor / by Susan Wels ; foreword by Senator Daniel K. Inouye ; introduction by Sir John Keegan.
p. cm.
"Tehabi books."
Includes bibliographical references and index.
ISBN 0-7370-0099-6
1. Pearl Harbor (Hawaii), Attack on, 1941. I. Title.

D767.92 .W46 2001
940.54'26—dc21
00-066637

The paper used in this publication meets the minimum requirements of the American National Standard for Information Sciences—Permanence of Paper for Printed Library Materials, ANSI Z39.48-1984.

Crippled ships

The battleship *California,* moored off Ford Island, lists to port after three torpedo hits while smoke billows from oil fires on the water.

Day of destruction

On Battleship Row, thick smoke from the burning *Arizona* and *West Virginia* surrounds the *Maryland* and the capsized *Oklahoma (right)*.

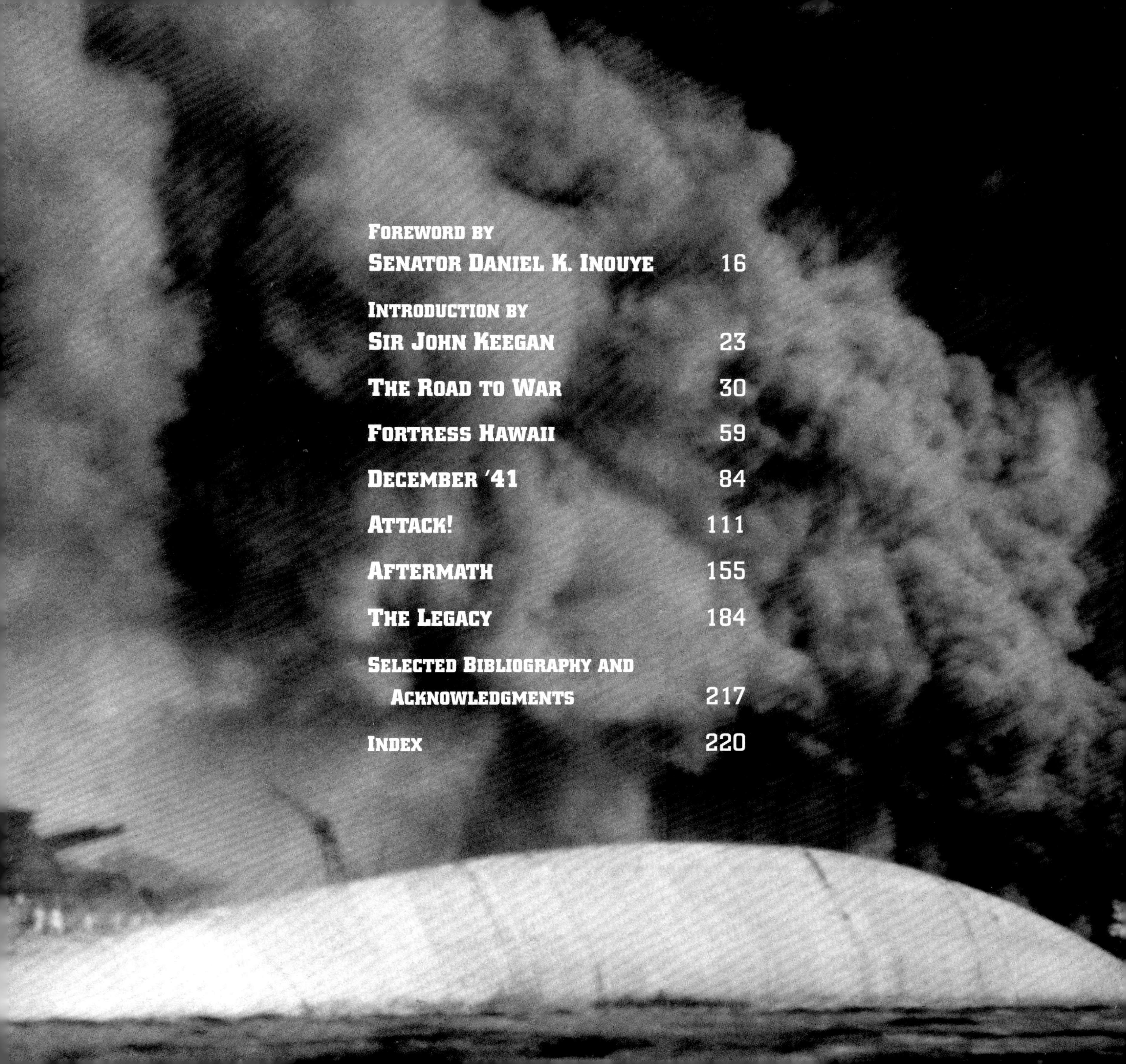

Foreword

BY SENATOR DANIEL K. INOUYE

It was a bright Sunday morning in December nearly six decades ago when aircraft bearing the symbol of the rising sun on their wings flew over my home in Hawaii. Upon hearing news of the attack over the radio, my father and I rushed outside, stood in the warm sunshine by the side of our house, and watched in horror as the planes climbed to the bluest part of the sky in neat formations of twos and threes, then dive-bombed and fired on the U.S. Pacific Fleet moored at Pearl Harbor. What had begun as a leisurely morning at breakfast and church had turned into a nightmare of blood and terror.

As we went back into the house, the secretary of the Red Cross telephoned to enlist my help, since I had recently begun teaching first aid. I immediately got on my bicycle and rushed to the aid station at my childhood school.

The station was more than a mile away from my home, and as I rode, I could see the fear and confusion in people's eyes and the devastation that those war planes wrought. By the time I reached the school, the first wave had ended. But the attack was far from over.

I found the Honolulu aid station in utter chaos. Everywhere people were shouting and pushing passed each other as they rushed for litters and medical supplies. Through all the noise and confusion, I could hear a voice droning from a radio somewhere. From one excited outburst from the announcer, I was able to glean that the USS *Arizona* had exploded, causing a great loss of life, and that other ships in the harbor had been badly damaged.

The other aides and I functioned on adrenaline and instinct. We set broken bones and dressed lacerations, working through the night and into the next day. Many civilians had, in fact, been wounded by our own anti-aircraft shells, which inadvertently fired without time fuses. Finding no target in the sky, the shells fell to the ground and exploded on impact, often inflicting terrible wounds and destruction. These casualties and those from the two waves of the attack mounted through the night. By the next morning, the school had become a morgue.

For the next several days, we tended to the sick, gave shelter to the homeless, and found food for the hungry. On the fifth day, I went home for the first time, filled with grief and shame, knowing that Japan, the land of my ancestors, had attacked America, my homeland, the country that I loved. I sensed that my world had come to an end. I was just seventeen years old.

Witness to disaster

As a seventeen-year-old student and first-aid teacher in Honolulu, Daniel K. Inouye—later a two-term U.S. Congressman and seven-term U.S. Senator—witnessed the devastating Japanese air strike at Pearl Harbor. After the raid, Inouye tended to many of the wounded, then enlisted in the army as a private in 1943.

I agree with those who have said that December 7 was the day the "sleeping giant awoke." After the attack, Americans everywhere rolled up their sleeves and joined the fight. Heroism, courage, and innovation were demonstrated on the battlefront and the home front as Americans rose to new heights of greatness and glory.

But December 7 was also the day that Americans began to see the ugly truth that ignorance and prejudice, now amplified by fear, were prevalent in our own country. The dark days that followed the attack were filled with anxiety for all Americans. This was especially true for Japanese Americans, who were deeply concerned about how their fellow Americans might treat them. Suspicions quickly arose about their allegiance to the United States. Soon Hawaii's Japanese Americans in the National Guard were discharged from duty, those in the Reserve Officers Training Corps and Territorial Guard were stripped of their weapons, and those already in the army were transferred to labor battalions.

Return to Pearl Harbor

Senator Inouye gazes out across Pearl Harbor, where the USS *Arizona* Memorial, in the background, was dedicated in 1962. Inouye lost his right arm in combat in 1945 while serving in Italy with the 442nd Regimental Combat Team, formed entirely of Americans of Japanese ancestry.

Our worst fears were realized when, in March 1942, the U.S. Army, under the authority of an executive order, forcibly moved about 110,000 Japanese Americans from the coastal Pacific states into relocation camps. Americans of Japanese ancestry had become "4-C" or "enemy aliens." This was a painful insult, since we considered ourselves law-abiding and loyal American citizens.

Fortunately for me and my family, the military leaders in Hawaii did not intern us. I was free to complete high school and to begin attending the University of Hawaii as a pre-med student. The military did, however, search my family's home after the bombing and destroyed our radio. We did not take our freedom for granted and frequently petitioned the authorities to give us an opportunity to prove that being an American was not a matter of skin color but rather a matter of heart.

In January 1943, a colonel in charge of the university's ROTC unit announced that the War Department had just decided to accept Japanese-American volunteers to join in forming a full-fledged combat team. I was initially turned down because I was considered essential as a worker at the medical-aid station and because I was enrolled in a pre-med course. I immediately gave my notice at the aid station and withdrew from the university. Two days later I was ordered to report for induction. More than a year after the attack on Pearl Harbor, 2,686 Japanese-American volunteers from Hawaii sailed off to war. I was number 2,685.

Before I left, my father, who had emigrated with his parents from Japan, said to me: "America has been good to us. You must return the goodness of this country at any cost. This is a matter of honor."

Lessons of war

As a member of Congress for more than forty years, Inouye was instrumental in bringing the battleship *Missouri* to Pearl Harbor as a permanent memorial. Commissioned on June 11, 1944, the *Missouri* was the vessel on which the Japanese formally surrendered to the United States in Tokyo Bay on September 2, 1945. Together with the *Arizona* shrine–honoring those killed in the first moments of the Pearl Harbor attack–the *Missouri* memorial commemorates the beginning and end of the Pacific War.

Because many of my peers had this same sense of honor instilled in them, we served our nation with courage and valor. The 100th Infantry Battalion and 442nd Regimental Combat Team were formed entirely from Nisei—second-generation Japanese Americans—who responded to the call for recruits. Together they became the most highly decorated unit of its size and length of service in the history of the U.S. military.

It is ironic that if Japan had not attacked Pearl Harbor, I might never have become a member of the U.S. Senate, where I have fought to avert war, maintain peace, promote racial harmony, and enhance diplomatic relations. On April 21, 1945, I lost my right arm during our unit's successful capture of a strategic hill while on a campaign in Italy, forcing me to give up my dream of becoming a surgeon. I turned my attention to politics and, with financial assistance from the G.I. bill, graduated from college and later earned a law degree, setting the stage for my forty-plus-year career as a member of Congress.

I will never forget that Sunday morning, and I hope that my fellow Americans will remember Pearl Harbor and its many lessons forever. To forget Pearl Harbor is to forget the good and evil that human beings are capable of in times of crisis. Without a vivid memory of this event, we may lack the fortitude and the preparedness to withstand future assaults on our country and its democratic ideals.

Dawn of war

A sailor races past the wreckage of hangars and seaplanes at Kaneohe Bay Naval Air Station near Pearl Harbor on December 7, 1941.

INTRODUCTION

BY SIR JOHN KEEGAN

President Franklin Delano Roosevelt, broadcasting to the American people at noon on December 8, 1941, told his audience, "Yesterday, the United States was suddenly and deliberately attacked by naval and air forces of the Empire of Japan." There had been no warning. Owing to unanticipated delays in transmission, the diplomatic ultimatum signaling Japan's intentions had not been delivered until after the surprise assault had taken place.

*The results were catastrophic. Of the eight battleships of the U.S. Pacific Fleet moored in Pearl Harbor, two—*Arizona *and* Oklahoma*—had been wrecked beyond repair. Another three—*West Virginia, Nevada, *and* California*—had been put out of action. Three more—*Maryland, Tennessee, *and* Pennsylvania, *the flagship—had also been damaged.*

Three light cruisers had been damaged, three destroyers sunk. Out of 394 aircraft on the island, 164 had been destroyed and 159 damaged; and 2,395 servicemen and civilians had been killed and another 1,178 wounded.

The Japanese attackers had scarcely suffered at all. None of Vice Admiral Chuichi Nagumo's six aircraft carriers had been touched, or even detected by the American defenders. Of the four hundred aircraft launched from them, only twenty-nine had been lost, some of them to accidents. The only significant American success was the sinking of two enemy midget submarines. The day of infamy, by every material index, had been a brilliant Japanese victory and a terrible American defeat.

Nagumo's returning aircrew, exultant at what they had achieved but eager to complete the victory, pressed for a renewed strike. The admiral felt he had done enough, even though none of the three American aircraft carriers, which were absent on independent missions, had been found. Unwilling to compromise his triumph, Nagumo turned his fleet away, to take part in Japan's developing war against American forces in the Philippines; the British in Malaya, Burma, and Hong Kong; and the Dutch in the Netherlands East Indies. By the middle of the coming year, all those territories and most of the islands of the western Pacific had fallen to the Japanese offensive.

Brass lantern used on ships

Japan's ruling class, and the Japanese people who took their view of the world from it, regarded the raid as a triumphant preliminary to a campaign of conquest throughout the European colonial

Shattered peace

The battleship *California,* moored alongside Ford Island in Pearl Harbor, was blasted by Japanese torpedoes and bombs. Ninety-eight crew members died on the ship during the attack. After sustaining severe flooding, the *California* sank to the bottom of the harbor on the evening of December 9.

possessions and American protectorates in Southeast Asia and the Pacific. The Japanese also believed the attack to be justified by the years of humiliation that they had suffered at the hands of the United States and the great European empires. Ever since their victory in the Russo-Japanese War of 1904–5, the Japanese found themselves frustrated in their efforts to create an empire of their own in the Far East. They had been forced to give up the spoils of victory in 1905, forced to accept subordinate status in the Anglo-American disarmament agreements following the First World War, and most recently, subjected to economic penalties for their attack on China in 1937.

As the only Asian people to have industrialized and modernized their country by their own efforts, the Japanese thought themselves entitled to leadership of the Asian world. Leadership, however, was to be on their terms, requiring control of the agricultural resources of China and the raw materials of Malaya, Burma, and the Netherlands East Indies. Their ambitions in China predestined conflict with the United States, which had early established itself as the sponsor of the young Chinese Republic's entry into the modern world. When, after 1937, Japan persisted in its aggression in China, America made its displeasure felt by denying Japan supplies of oil and strategic metals. By late 1941 Japan had decided that American economic constriction could be raised only by the challenge of war.

The immediate results of going to war appeared to justify the risk. The Japanese navy, with the army following in its wake, defeated

Vulnerable vessel

The *California* was especially vulnerable to torpedo attacks and flooding because her watertight compartments were wide open, in preparation for a scheduled inspection. After bombs exploded the battleship's ammunition magazines, flames from burning oil engulfed the vessel, and her captain ordered the crew to abandon ship. Although the battleship began listing dangerously to port, successful counterflooding measures kept the *California* from capsizing.

the British and Dutch navies in eastern waters, inflicted further reverses on the U.S. Navy, and captured the Philippines, Malaya, Burma and the Dutch East Indies, to add to the conquests already made in China and to the occupation of French Indo-China. By May 1942, Japan's armed forces appeared invincible in their chosen area of operations.

As Nagumo had identified, however, in the aftermath of his Pearl Harbor strike, his victory had not been complete. The aircraft carriers of the U.S. Pacific Fleet, absent on detached missions, had escaped attack. They were now to reappear, with dramatic and eventually decisive consequences for the outcome of the Pacific War.

During February and March, the carriers *Enterprise, Saratoga,* and *Lexington,* based in Pearl Harbor and refueling from its undamaged stores of 4.5 million barrels of oil and high-octane gasoline, launched strikes against newly acquired Japanese bases in the Gilbert and Solomon Islands and against Wake Island, which had been heroically defended by American Marines until they were overwhelmed in December. None of these carrier strikes succeeded in blunting the Japanese onset. In April, however, the U.S. Navy conceived a carrier mission that gravely unsettled the Japanese high command's state of mind. Deciding to strike directly at the seat of Japanese power, navy crews loaded sixteen B-25 land bombers onto the USS *Hornet,* from which they flew eight hundred miles to attack four Japanese cities, including Tokyo. The crews, which could not return to the carriers, then flew on

to crash-land on the Asian mainland. All but five of the aircrew survived.

This direct affront to the safety of the Japanese emperor caused Japan's military leaders to abandon their plans to enlarge their conquests in Southeast Asia. Instead they decided to extend their area of oceanic control, so as to ensure that the Americans could never again strike at the Japanese home islands. The attack on Tokyo had wounded their honor as the defenders of the emperor's person.

The Japanese leadership identified the island of New Guinea, north of Australia, as the key location. If captured, it would prevent the United States from using Australia as a strategic base for

Attack from above

Hours after the attack on Pearl Harbor, survivors look skyward for the return of Japanese planes. Expecting the enemy to strike again, sailors made a machine-gun pit from piled sand bags on this Ford Island seaplane ramp. Across the harbor, the damaged battleship *Nevada* is grounded at Waipio Peninsula.

the continuation of the naval war. On May 7, 1942, a Japanese carrier force fought an American carrier fleet off New Guinea in the Battle of the Coral Sea. Tactically a stalemate, strategically it was an American victory. The Japanese, having set out to win outright naval victory in the Pacific by the surprise attack on Pearl Harbor, now found themselves committed to a conventional struggle for supremacy in fleet action. Unless they could find and destroy the American carriers, further attacks on the home islands would follow, to their dishonor and long-term disadvantage.

The crux came at Midway, on June 4. The Americans, determined to bring the Japanese carriers to battle, had laid an elaborate trap around Midway, the last surviving American island close to Japan. Believing Midway to be undefended, Nagumo brought the six carriers that had devastated Pearl Harbor into a position from which a landing could be launched. He had six carriers; Admiral Spruance had three, the veteran *Enterprise,* together with the *Yorktown* and the *Hornet*. The Americans, however, had the benefit of superior intelligence, derived from their ability to read Japanese ciphers. They were aware of Nagumo's location; he was ignorant of their presence. After an initial encounter, in which the Japanese destroyed all the attacking American torpedo bombers, three of Nagumo's surviving carriers were sunk by dive-bombing. A fourth was sunk later in the day.

Midway was the revenge for Pearl Harbor and a defeat from which the Imperial Japanese Navy never recovered. The core of its carrier fleet had been sunk and with it most of its superb naval air force. Neither ships nor aircraft nor pilots would ever be replaced. The Americans, by contrast, were already launching the first of dozens of the superlative new *Essex*-class carriers, which, by the summer of 1945, were carrying the Pacific naval war to the outliers of the Japanese home islands. It was an outcome that should have been foreseen. In the last years of peace, Admiral Yamamoto, the architect of the Pearl Harbor attack but also a former naval attaché in Washington, had warned his army colleagues, who controlled the government, that "we can run wild for a year or six months." After that, he said, the power of America's mighty industry would prevail. It was a prediction of awesome accuracy.

The consequences, disastrous as they were for Americans and the Japanese, cannot detract from the interest of the story, recounted here with dramatic effect by Susan Wels. Public interest in the attack and its implications remains unabated. Why did the Japanese persuade themselves that they could permanently reverse the balance of advantage in the Pacific by a single strike? How did the Americans fail to detect it? Did Roosevelt have foreknowledge? Whatever else is to be said about it, Pearl Harbor was and remains one of the great events of history, driving all other news from the page and coming to stand eventually as a metaphor for totally unexpected action.

Destroyed aircraft
At Kaneohe Bay Naval Air Station on the eastern tip of Oahu, crews push a damaged PBY seaplane away from burning wreckage after the attack. Twenty-seven of the air base's thirty-three seaplanes were destroyed, and another six were badly damaged. Japanese fighter and bomber planes struck Kaneohe Bay during the first and second waves of the assault.

Battleship Row

The warships on Battleship Row—*(from right to left)* the burning *Arizona,* the *Tennessee,* and the *West Virginia*—were the main targets of the Japanese attack.

Bursting from the clouds, swarms of Japanese planes blasted the Sunday-morning stillness of Oahu with a thundering fury of explosions, guns, and flame. In two hours of destruction, on December 7, 1941, the surprise attack on U.S. bases on Oahu and at Pearl Harbor took the lives of nearly twenty-four hundred Americans and crippled the U.S. Pacific Fleet. Japanese attacks were simultaneously sweeping across the Pacific from Wake Island, Midway, and Guam to the Philippines, Malaya, and Hong Kong.

For Americans—clinging to peace, yet slipping steadily toward war—the moment of decision had arrived. The next day, President Franklin D. Roosevelt asked the House and Senate to declare war on the Empire of Japan. "There is no blinking at the fact that our people, our territory, and our interests are in grave danger," he warned; December 7, 1941, was "a date which will live in infamy."

THE ROAD TO WAR

The attack climaxed a decade that had swept much of Europe, Asia, and Africa into war. Many Americans believed that the United States was immune to forces that were convulsing nations overseas, and they had struggled to stay out of the widening conflict. But Pearl Harbor, a stunning strike launched while America and Japan were still at peace, shocked the nation from its isolationist torpor. Four days later, Japan's allies, Germany and Italy, declared war on the United States. Once reluctant to fight, Americans were now galvanized in their resolve to avenge Pearl Harbor and defeat the Axis powers. "The only thing now," raged Senator Burton K. Wheeler (D-Montana), an outspoken isolationist, "is to do our best to lick hell out of them."

Day of infamy

On December 8, 1941—the day after the Pearl Harbor attack—President Roosevelt addressed a joint session of the U.S. House and Senate, asking Congress to declare war on Japan. The Senate unanimously approved the president's request. In the House, only one member, Representative Jeannette Rankin (R-Montana), voted against the declaration. Rankin had also voted against U.S. participation in the First World War.

Roosevelt cautioned America that it would be "a long war . . . a hard war." In truth, the Second World War would be the most terrible, costly war in all of history. Some fifty million people died in six years of worldwide devastation, and its ending brought the anxious dawning of the atomic age. It was, as Adolf Hitler said, "one of those elemental conflicts . . . which shakes the world once in a thousand years." And the seeds of its savagery were sown in the aftermath of the First World War, the war that the world believed would end all future wars.

In 1919, in negotiations at the close of the Great War, three victor nations—the United States and the Allied countries of Britain and France—dictated an uneasy peace through the terms of the Treaty of Versailles. Although Italy had fought with the Allies, against the will of its

own people, it received few of the lands it had been promised by the victors. And although Japan, also an Ally, left Versailles as a world power, the peace conference was marked by racial conflict. Germany, declared the aggressor, was disarmed, stripped of her colonies, and punished with burdensome war reparations. Defeated and bitter, Germany plunged into economic chaos. From 1918 to 1923, the value of the German mark declined a billion times, from 4 to 130 million to the dollar.

In Italy and Germany, instability and unemployment swelled the ranks of the burgeoning Fascist and Nazi movements, factions that promised glory, prosperity, and pride under militaristic, authoritarian systems. Benito Mussolini and his black-shirted Fascist supporters seized control of the Italian government in 1922, installing a repressive, totalitarian regime. In 1929, America's stock market crash further shook the economies of Europe. Adolf Hitler, leader of the ascendant Nazi party, took power in Germany in 1933, silencing dissidents, purging Germany of Jews to purify the Nordic "master race," and threatening to rebuild his military into the most powerful war machine in Europe to avenge his nation's treatment at Versailles.

In the mid-1930s, while a third of Americans were still, in Roosevelt's words, "ill-housed, ill-clothed, ill-nourished," Britain and France were also struggling through economic crisis. Shunning conflict after the agonies of the First World War, they turned inward, withdrawing from international affairs. They did nothing to stop Hitler when his

Rise of the Third Reich

Defeated in the Great War and embittered by the Treaty of Versailles, many Germans, especially former members of the military, were attracted to the growing Nazi Party. In 1921, Adolf Hitler, *left,* rose to power as the Nazi Party leader in Bavaria. Denouncing Communists and Jews for conspiring against the German people, Hitler expanded Nazism's popular support and was named Germany's chancellor in January 1933. Two months later, backed by violent squads of Nazi storm troopers, he seized power as dictator. *Right,* German Stug III assault gun.

troops flouted the Treaty of Versailles in 1936 by marching into the Rhineland, an area demilitarized after the war as a buffer zone between the Rhine River and France. When Nazi infantry and artillery battalions, brashly sporting red carnations, paraded into Cologne and the surrounding Rhineland region, they defiantly reclaimed Germany's prewar territory. The Allies, Hitler promised, had nothing to fear; Germany, he declared, had "no territorial demands to make in Europe."

Months later, Germany tested its growing military might in the erupting civil war in Spain. Hitler's planes gave General Francisco Franco and his Fascist rebels control of Spanish airspace, and Mussolini backed Franco's Nationalist forces with matériel and troops. Then, in March 1938, Nazi soldiers and tanks pushed across the border into Austria to enforce *Anschluss,* the incorporation of that country into the German Reich. As swastika flags rose over the Hofburg Palace in Vienna and storm troopers seized Austrian dissidents, the Allied nations once again stood by and watched. Nothing could have stopped this move by Germany, conceded Britain's prime minister, Neville Chamberlain, "unless we and others with us had been prepared to use force to prevent it."

There were no protests either from Italy, Austria's neighbor. Since October 1935,

Asserting power
In September 1938, Hitler and the head of his Gestapo, Heinrich Himmler, review SS troops during Reich Party Day ceremonies in Nuremburg.

Mussolini's government had pursued its own territorial ambitions, attacking Ethiopia in hopes of establishing a Fascist Roman Empire in Africa. In October 1936, Mussolini and Hitler had formally aligned their regimes by forging a strategic "axis" linking Berlin with Rome. Now, with Hitler's invasion of Austria, that axis was a physical fact, an unbroken stretch of Nazi- and Fascist-dominated territory reaching from the Mediterranean to the Baltic.

Emboldened, Hitler eyed new acquisitions to the east. Germany's borders now surrounded Czechoslovakia on three sides, and on September 12, 1938, Hitler moved to close the gap by menacing the Czech Sudetenland, a region with a majority of more than three million pro-Nazi German speakers. Neither France nor Britain was militarily or psychologically prepared to fight to help the threatened Czechs. Instead, their leaders, Chamberlain and French Prime Minister Edouard Daladier, traveled to Munich to try to prevent war through a negotiated settlement. The Munich agreement they brokered at the end of September was a triumph for Hitler, dismembering Czechoslovakia and giving him the prize of the Sudetenland. While Chamberlain and Daladier congratulated themselves on persuading the Nazis to negotiate instead of waging war, others around the world were growing uneasy with their appeasement strategy of "peace at any price." As former premier of France Léon Blum acknowledged, "War has probably been averted, but I feel myself divided between cowardly relief [and a] sense of shame."

Despite his one-sided diplomatic victory in Munich, Hitler abruptly shattered the accord in March 1939. Nazi troops and tanks moved swiftly to invade the rest of Czechoslovakia, rolling into Prague as Czechs wept in the streets and radios blasted warnings that "the slightest resistance will bring . . . utter brutality." The Allies, stunned by this aggression, were blindsided yet again. On August 23, Hitler's Reich surprised the world by announcing

Peace at any price

At the Hotel Dreesen, *left,* in Bad Godesberg, Germany, British Prime Minister Neville Chamberlain met with Adolf Hitler on September 22, 1938. Chamberlain agreed to let Hitler seize the German-speaking Czech Sudetenland in order to prevent war with Germany.

Axis allies

On May 22, 1939, Italy's dictator, Benito Mussolini, and Hitler, *below,* forged a "Pact of Steel," binding their nations militarily with the goal of redrawing the political map of Europe.

the signing of a pact with its ideological nemesis, Communist Russia. Endangered by this new alliance was the isolated nation of Poland, surrounded by territory-hungry Germany on its western flank and the Soviets on its eastern border. Although Britain had guaranteed Poland's security in March, the country had now become virtually impossible to defend. In fact, Germany and Russia had, in secret negotiations, made plans to divide Polish territory between them.

Acting quickly to preempt a British and French move, Hitler launched a blitzkrieg on Poland in the early hours of September 1. Two days later, on September 3, 1939, Britain and France declared war on Germany—officially commencing the Second World War—but Poland's fate was already determined. A million and a half Nazi troops advanced inexorably across Poland, crushing the country's disorganized and poorly equipped army with their invincible Panzer tank columns; the Soviets invaded from the east on September 17. A fierce new Nazi weapon—the Stuka dive bomber—relentlessly droned over Warsaw, bombarding the capital in accordance with orders to destroy "everything living or standing." By September 28, when at last Warsaw surrendered, it was a "dead city" that stank of burning flesh.

Polish resistance ended on October 5. Enriched by Polish spoils, the Soviets acted to guard their Baltic flank by annexing the Baltic

War begins

Nazi troops, tanks, and dive bombers invaded Poland on September 1, 1939. Two days later, Britain and France declared war on Germany, igniting the Second World War in Europe. On September 28, the Polish people surrendered to Hitler's forces.

states and invading Finland. Then, on April 9, 1940, Germany launched an offensive into Scandinavia, quickly swallowing the Kingdom of Denmark, then battling the Allies for control of Norway. Hitler struck again on May 10, driving into the neutral countries of Holland, Luxembourg, and Belgium, seizing positions from which to attack the French army and the British Expeditionary Force.

Within sixty days, France, too, was overwhelmed. A crushing onslaught of fierce Panzer divisions and Stuka air attacks immobilized France's two-and-a-half-million-man army and forced the evacuation of the British Expeditionary Force from Dunkirk, while the *Luftwaffe* outgunned the French *Armée de l'Air* and Britain's Royal Air Force. On June 14, battle-stained Nazi tanks and armored motorcycles triumphantly roared through the deserted streets of Paris, and on June 22, the French Third Republic signed a humiliating armistice with Adolf Hitler. Defeated by "the gods of force and hate," as Roosevelt described Hitler's offensive, the new French government retained control of only the southern sector of the country. The Battle of France was over; now, as British Prime Minister Winston Churchill predicted, the Battle of Britain was about to begin.

The London Blitz

Hitler launched his first mass air attack on London on September 7, 1940, targeting docklands on the river Thames, *right*. In eight hours of bombing that day, some fifteen hundred Nazi planes dropped 4.4 million pounds of explosives on the city, blasting oil tanks, docks, munitions, and electrical and water supplies.

Hitler's triumph

After their blitzkrieg conquest of France in June 1940, the first battle-seasoned columns of Nazi troops return, triumphant, to the German capital of Berlin, parading proudly through the city's Brandenburg Gate, *below*.

The first phase of Hitler's cross-Channel assault on Britain, in July and August 1940, was an intense aerial attack on southern ports and military and radar installations to prepare for a planned amphibious invasion. The *Luftwaffe,* with more than twenty-five hundred planes, outnumbered Britain's one thousand fighters, but Germany failed to overcome Britain's air defenses. On September 7, to crush her morale, Hitler launched "the Blitz," devastating day and night air attacks on London. Waves of German planes rained bombs onto the city's docklands, igniting fires that were explosively stoked by later raids. Despite the incessant destruction and loss of life, Londoners and the RAF's Fighter Command carried on. By the end of September, the *Luftwaffe* was sustaining heavy losses, and Hitler was suffering his first military defeat.

Safely across the Atlantic Ocean, Americans watched as Europe's democracies, one after another, collapsed in the face of Hitler's onslaughts. Despite the grave news from overseas, however, the United States was unwilling to send its soldiers to fight Hitler in Europe. Americans had been suffering from deprivation and unemployment for a decade. Although President

The Holocaust begins
Nazi SS officials confer during a prisoners' roll call at Buchenwald, one of the first Nazi concentration camps. Jews and other "racial enemies" were imprisoned as slave laborers. Many were executed, and others died from starvation, disease, and as victims of brutal medical experiments.

Roosevelt's New Deal policies had raised morale, millions of Americans—15 percent of the labor force—were still out of work, and a strong mood of isolationism gripped the country. Americans, secure inside their continental borders and focused on domestic struggles, paid little heed to global tensions. Many were disillusioned with the high ideals that had sent thousands of young American soldiers off to war in 1917. "We were all suckers," declared one disabled soldier in a cynical 1936 ad financed by an isolationist group. Encouraged by Senate investigations of arms makers and international bankers, many Americans blamed these "merchants of death" for dragging the nation into the First World War.

Through most of the 1930s, President Roosevelt, reflecting these sentiments, starved the military budget and shunned what he termed "political commitments which might entangle us in foreign wars." The army, forced to rely on outdated equipment, was reduced to a corps smaller than that of Bulgaria or Greece. In addition, to keep the United States from entering armed conflicts, Congress passed neutrality laws strictly forbidding loans to belligerents or trade with any party in a war. As the situation

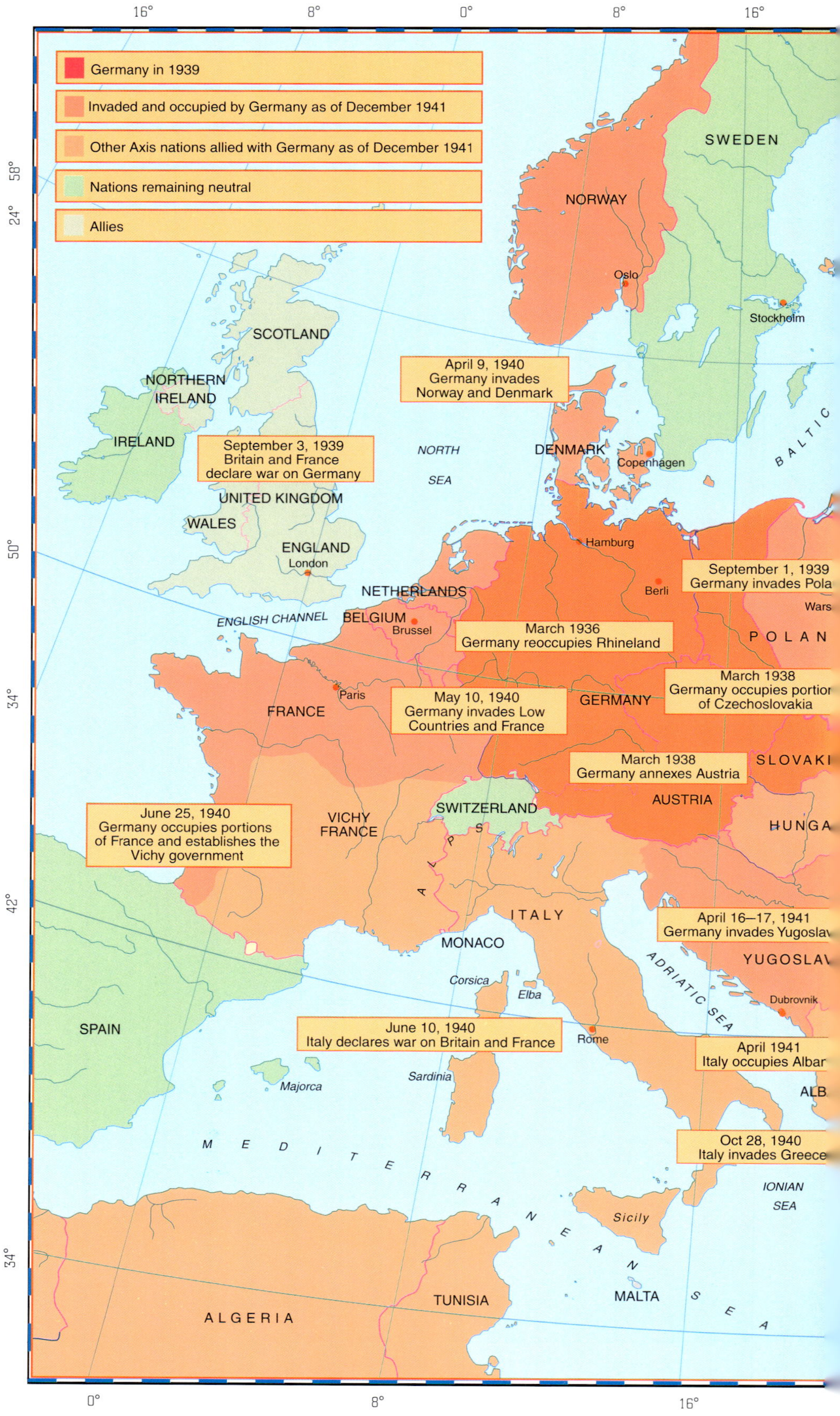

German conquests in Europe

After Germany reoccupied the Rhineland in 1936 in defiance of the Treaty of Versailles, Hitler launched a policy of expansion in Europe to acquire *lebensraum,* new territories for German occupation. In 1938, Germany annexed Austria and the Czech Sudetenland. The next year, Hitler seized the rest of Czechoslovakia and invaded Poland. In 1940, Nazi forces occupied Denmark and Norway, then began a blitzkrieg through western Europe, invading the Netherlands, Belgium, and then France. By July 1941, Hitler had overrun the Balkans, and his forces had advanced into Soviet territory.

Depression-era America

In the United States, New Deal programs such as the Civilian Conservation Corps (CCC), *far left,* put the unemployed to work during the Great Depression.

worsened overseas, however, Roosevelt searched for a way to respond to global aggression while keeping America at peace. He persuaded Congress to authorize the "cash-and-carry" sale of U.S. armaments to Britain and France in 1939. Then, in 1940, after France collapsed and Britain came under Hitler's siege, he mobilized the United States to assist the British in every possible manner "short of war." America, he insisted, could not become "a lone island in a world dominated by the philosophy of force."

Still, America's military remained disastrously weak. In September 1938, a German report noted that the United States had "no military preparations whatever nor any measures for setting industrial mobilization in motion." In September 1939, while the Nazis were storming across Poland, Roosevelt assured the country that "there is no thought in any shape, manner or form, of putting the Nation, either in its defenses or in its internal economy, on a war basis." But after the fall of France in June 1940, Congress approved a massive budget to rearm and to provide crucial aid to allies overseas; in September, the United States initiated its first peacetime military draft. Although more than 70 percent of the American public supported the

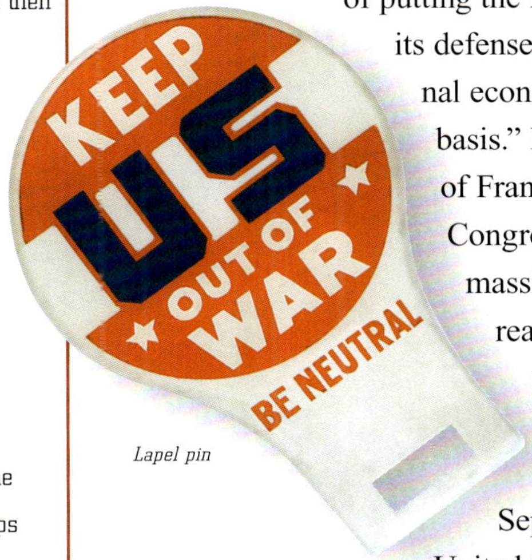

Lapel pin

draft measure, isolationists decried Roosevelt as a "warmonger," and hundreds of citizens' committees voiced outrage at what they interpreted as America's steady steps toward war.

Faced with this intense national debate, and in the middle of his third campaign for president, Roosevelt was ambivalent about the U.S. military role. "I shall say it again and again and again," he told supporters in October 1940. "Your boys are not going to be sent into any foreign wars." Despite its stepped-up aid to Germany's enemies, most believed that the United States would manage to avoid entering the European conflict. America "may be sick with pity" for the victims of totalitarian aggression in Europe, as *Harper's Magazine* put it, "but we are thankful we are out of it" and "hardly afraid of being dragged in."

Staying out of war

Since its early days, the United States sought to avoid "entangling alliances" with other countries. At the end of the First World War, Americans rejected the League of Nations and the Treaty of Versailles, signaling their desire to stay out of international affairs. Hearings led by Senator Gerald P. Nye led to the passage of Neutrality Acts in 1935 and 1937 that restricted U.S. aid to belligerent nations. By 1940, powerful pressure groups such as the America First Committee actively opposed American military involvement in Europe. President Roosevelt, running for a third term and sensitive to the country's mood, pledged that Americans would not send their sons to fight in foreign conflicts.

Many Americans, however, were growing less confident about avoiding an armed clash on another front, in the Pacific. In the 1930s, Japan had increasingly emerged as an enemy of American interests in Asia. Lacking vital supplies of food and raw materials and hard hit by the worldwide depression, Japan saw itself, in the years after the First World War, as a "have-not" nation denied the opportunity—unlike the great powers of Europe—to enrich itself through territorial expansion. Since then, the Western powers had sought to rein in Japan's ambitions for new territories. But, needing crucial resources such as metal, rubber, and oil, Tokyo, under the rising influence of ultranationalist military leaders, embarked on a policy of conquest on the Chinese continent to ensure supply.

In September 1931, Japanese troops seized the city of Mukden in the rich northern Chinese region of Manchuria. The United States, led by Secretary of State Henry Stimson, vigorously denounced the aggression. Americans had long seen themselves as China's protectors, guarding its "Open Door" to foreign trade. But in the throes of global depression, neither the United States nor any other nation came to China's defense. China itself, torn between battling Communist and Nationalist forces, allowed Japan to maintain control over Manchuria through the puppet government of Manchukuo.

Lindbergh's "Appeal for Isolation"

September 15, 1939

A month after celebrated aviator Charles A. Lindbergh returned to the United States following a three-year stay in Europe, he broadcast a speech, excerpted below, over America's radio networks. The Second World War had just begun in Europe, after Hitler's invasion of Poland on September 1. Sympathetic to the Nazis and hoping to keep America out of war, Lindbergh, with this speech, began forcefully challenging President Roosevelt, his ideological opponent, in the battle for public opinion.

I speak tonight to those people of the United States of America who feel that the destiny of this country does not call for our involvement in European wars. . . .

Modern war with all its consequences is too tragic and too devastating to be approached from anything but a purely American standpoint. We should never enter a war unless it is absolutely essential to the future welfare of our nation. . . .

These wars in Europe are not wars in which our civilization is defending itself against some Asiatic intruder. There is no Genghis Khan nor Xerxes marching against our Western nations. This is not a question of banding together to defend the white race against foreign invasion. This is simply . . . a quarrel arising from the errors of the last war—from the failure of the victors of that war to follow a consistent policy either of fairness or of force. . . .

America has little to gain by taking part in another European war. We must not be misguided by this foreign propaganda to the effect that our frontiers lie in Europe. One only need glance at a map to see where our true frontiers lie. What more could we ask than the Atlantic Ocean on the east and the Pacific on the west? No, our interests in Europe need not be from the standpoint of defense. Our own natural frontiers are enough for that. If we extend them at all, we might as well extend them around the earth. An ocean is a formidable barrier, even for modern aircraft.

Our safety does not lie in fighting European wars. It lies in our own internal strength, in the character of the American people and of American institutions. As long as we maintain an army, a navy and an air force worthy of the name, as long as America does not decay within, we need fear no invasion of this country.

Spirit of isolationism

Celebrated as "Lucky Lindy," Charles A. Lindbergh was famed for his historic nonstop flight in 1927 across the Atlantic from New York to Paris. In 1936, he and his wife, Ann Morrow Lindbergh, moved to Europe. The famous flier admired Hitler's aviation program and was awarded a medal by the Nazis. After returning to the United States in 1939, he began speaking out in support of isolationism, striving to keep America out of the war in Europe. In August 1938, Lindbergh, *above right,* meets with Nazi officials in Germany. *Left,* Lindbergh *(second from right)* inspects a U.S. Boeing F2B-1 in 1929 with pilot Jimmy Doolittle (arms crossed), who years later staged a daring air raid on Tokyo.

In July 1937, however, Japan's occupation of China turned into outright war when Japanese troops deliberately provoked a clash with Chinese troops outside Peking.

Determined to resist Japan's assaults, Chinese Nationalists and Communists joined together to form a fighting front, but Japan—with extremist military leaders firmly in control of the government—met Chinese resistance with brutal force, massacring the civilian population of Nanking and seizing some half-million square miles of China. With twelve hundred fighting planes and hundreds of thousands of well-armed troops, Japan had the military edge. Still, the Japanese were faced with the difficulties of transporting and supplying a large and distant garrison in China, whereas the Chinese were fighting on home soil, with the advantages of their vast population and resources. The Chinese continued to resist, despite their suffering, pinning down Japanese troops in a desperate, seemingly unwinnable conflict.

As the war between Japan and China escalated, the United States, Britain, and the Soviet Union vigorously condemned the Tokyo government for its expansionist policies.

Imperial aggression

Japanese soldiers, *left,* take aim on the steps of a church in the Chapei section of Shanghai.

Chinese resistance

Japan's 280,000-man garrison, in China—fully trained and well equipped—battled a vast Chinese army, *right,* of two million soldiers, poorly armed but fighting on their home territory.

The Tripartite Pact

On September 27, 1940, German Foreign Minister Joachim von Ribbentrop, *below,* addresses dignitaries at the signing of the Tripartite Pact, an agreement that linked Japan, Germany, and Italy as Axis allies.

Japan's ultranationalist leaders, however, were determined to secure their nation's standing as a rich, industrial world power through a strategy of territorial conquest. Increasingly, they envisioned Japan as the leader of a "New Order in East Asia," free of Western influence, that stretched from Manchukuo to other regions rich with vital resources in China, the Dutch East Indies, French Indochina, and the southwestern Pacific Ocean.

In June 1940, Japan saw an opportunity to gain a long-sought-after foothold in Southeast Asia. Since the Netherlands and France were under the control of Germany, with whom Japan had signed the Anti-Comintern Pact in 1936, their Asian colonies were now vulnerable to Japan. Tokyo accordingly demanded permission from the recently defeated French government to construct air bases in French Indochina and transport troops through the territory. France's leaders acquiesced, and on September 22, Japanese forces began pouring into northern Indochina. Five days later, Japan cemented its alliance with Hitler by signing the Tripartite Pact with Germany and Italy. The accord pledged the three Axis powers to assist each other in the event of an attack by another nation; it declared "the leadership of Germany and Italy in the establishment of a new order in Europe" and recognized the leadership of Japan in creating a "new order in Greater East Asia."

Advance into China

In August 1937, a month after the Sino-Japanese War began, Japanese troops battled Chinese forces outside Peking. By the middle of 1938, Japan controlled most of the principal cities in northern China.

A typhoon could not have done more damage to Japan's relations with the United States, as a former Japanese premier observed. Long sympathetic to China and outraged at Japanese aggression, Americans now looked at Japan as a "predatory power" and potential enemy. Its alliance with the Axis, wrote Robert Aura Smith of the *New York Times,* "has done more than anything else could have . . . to convince Americans that the war in Europe and the war in Asia are the same war"; in this atmosphere, he asserted, American aid to China is "not merely an affront to Tokyo—it is a blow at Berlin." President Roosevelt responded by authorizing a $100 million loan to the Chinese and stepped up economic pressure on Japan. America was by far Japan's biggest supplier of vital war matériel, including scrap iron and steel, oil, gasoline, pig iron, copper, machinery, engines, automobiles, and trucks—resources that were essential to Japan's military machine.

The United States had begun using its economic influence to restrain Japan in July 1938, restricting its purchases of airplanes and parts. In July 1940, Roosevelt had also banned sales of high-grade scrap metal, machine tools, and aviation fuel. Now, in September, Roosevelt responded to Japan's Indochinese advance by embargoing brass, copper, and iron sales, then added to the list of restricted materials every month. Still, the president stopped short of barring Japanese purchases of oil, fearful that it would force Japan to go to war to meet its critical fuel needs.

Wartime shortages

As Japan's war with China escalated, the country's standard of living fell sharply. To increase Japanese arms production, labor was diverted from agriculture and fishing, resulting in widespread food shortages.

The two countries found themselves at a strategic impasse. American policy makers were determined to contain Japan and restore China's territorial integrity. Japan was equally set on following a self-determined course and pursuing its own policy in China. By November 1940, with crucial supplies cut off and forced to meet the demands of its military garrison in China, Japan was under increasing economic strain. Standards of living had dropped 40 percent, nutrition was suffering, and even the availability of essentials such as clothing fell. With dwindling supplies of restricted foreign cotton, the Japanese government urged the manufacture of clothing made from *sufu,* a fragile fiber manufactured from lumber, which disintegrated rapidly. Car owners were encouraged to install charcoal gas generators in their vehicles as gasoline supplies dwindled. Even so, by the end of 1940 charcoal was nearly as hard to find as gasoline, and the nation was enduring severe shortages of fuel for heating, cooking, production, and transport.

Japan's deteriorating conditions were clear to John K. Emmerson, a U.S. Foreign Service officer in Tokyo. "The evidence of food, fuel,

and clothing shortages was all around us," he remembered. Necessities were rationed, and private automobiles were even converted into wood-burners. "Taxi drivers," he recalled, "would stop their cars, go to the back, and stoke the fire in the compartment where the trunk had been." All the while, citizens prepared for war with air raid drills, hung black curtains on the windows of their flammable wooden houses, performed early-morning calisthenics in the streets, and waved white flags while sending their sons and brothers off to war. "These observations confirmed, if confirmation was needed," Emmerson noted, "the 'realities' of Japan's vulnerability and total dependence on the outside world for essential raw materials."

Planning the attack

Japanese Admiral Isoroku Yamamoto believed that his country would not be able to win a long-term war against the United States. Once Japan's leaders had resolved to go to war, however, Yamamoto calculated that a surprise strike against the U.S. Pacific Fleet would give Japan its best chance of success.

Shocked by U.S. sanctions and fearful of ever-worsening conditions, Japan's leaders became increasingly determined to "take military actions in southern areas" to gain resources and win the war in China; the conquest of Southeast Asia, they expected, would eventually be "a matter of life and death." In December 1940, sensing Japan's rising desperation, Joseph Grew, America's ambassador to Japan, drafted a letter to President Roosevelt. The United States, he predicted grimly, was bound, sooner or later, "to come to a head-on clash with Japan."

JAPAN'S IMPERIAL AGGRESSION

On September 18, 1931, officers in Japan's Manchurian Kwantung Army, acting on their own initiative, blew up a section of the South Manchurian Railway and blamed the attack on Chinese soldiers. Japanese troops, seizing the opportunity, then moved quickly to capture the Chinese city of Mukden. Within months, they controlled all of the resource-rich northern region of Manchuria.

Japan's leaders welcomed the "Manchurian Incident." The country had been hit hard by world-wide depression and American tariffs. Vital silk exports declined, production fell, and farm income dropped by 40 percent. With shrinking exports, Japan feared it would be unable to buy the resources it needed from abroad. The solution, argued Tokyo's increasingly powerful military faction, was for Japan to seize the raw resources it coveted in Asia, enhancing its economic independence and strategic power.

With its promising supplies of coal, oil, iron, and shale, Manchuria was central to Japan's rebuilding efforts. Economic plans were threatened, however, in January 1932 when resistant Chinese began boycotting Japanese goods. To quash the boycott, Japan sent a powerful naval force to the international city of Shanghai to burn and rampage

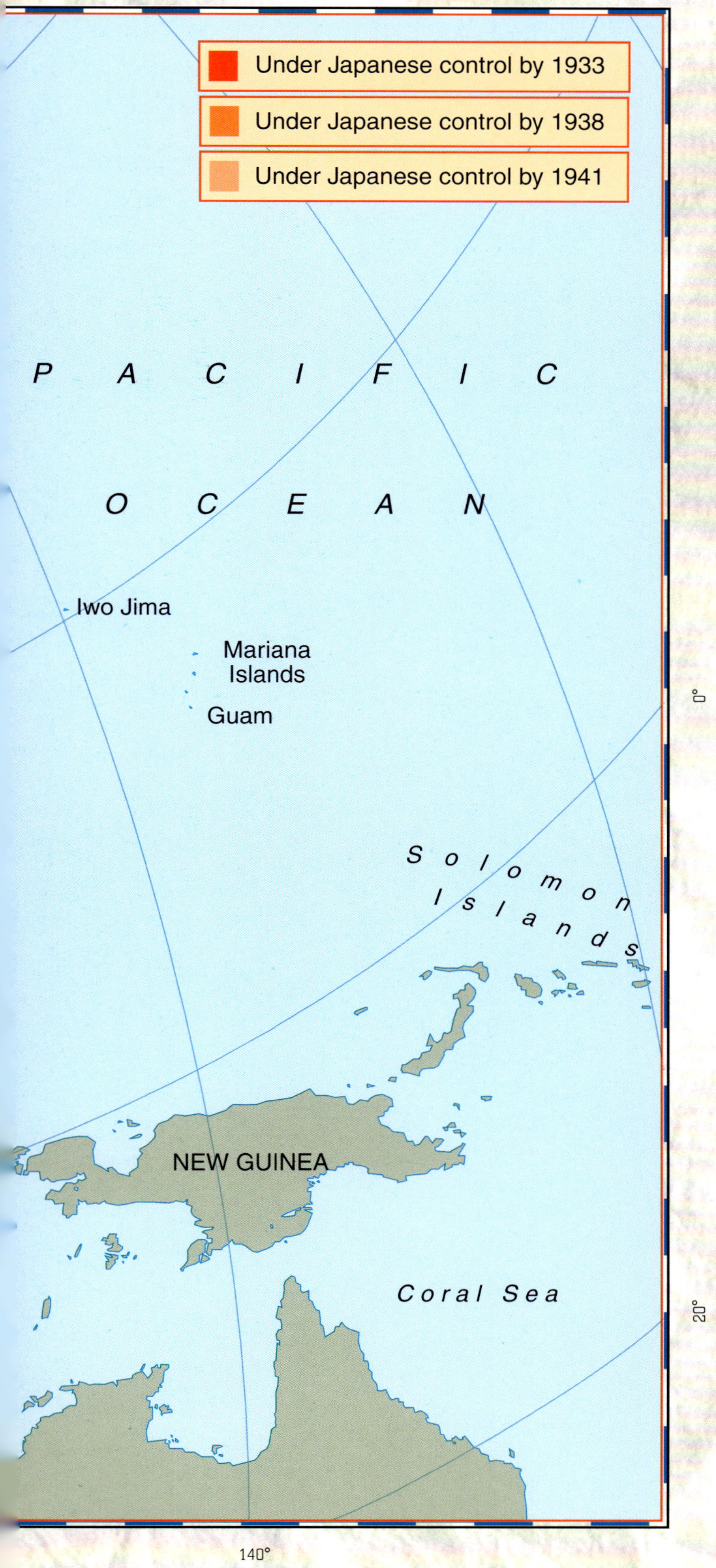

Occupation of China

In October 1931, a month after the "Manchurian Incident," soldiers in Japan's Kwangtung Army, *below,* watch the burning of the Manchurian city of Changtu. From 1931 to 1941, *left,* Japanese forces advanced across China, occupying major cities including Mukden, Shanghai, Canton, Hankow, and Nanking.

through Chapei, the city's Chinese quarter. The next month, Japan turned Manchuria into its puppet colony of Manchukuo, installing Henry Pu-yi, the last emperor in China's Manchu Dynasty, as its nominal head.

As Japanese garrisons tightened their grip on China, attitudes in the West began to harden against Japan. Meanwhile, Japan's military faction increasingly asserted power and assassinated moderate opponents. In 1933, after the League of Nations denounced the occupation of Manchuria, Japan responded by withdrawing its delegation from the league.

In China, victorious troops of the Kwantung Army garrison continued to take matters into their own hands. By 1935, with their numbers swollen to 164,000 soldiers, they made regular, unauthorized incursions into Inner Mongolia and China. Finally, on the night of July 7, 1937, Japanese troops

sparked a second far-reaching "incident." On maneuvers near Peking, they exchanged fire with Chinese soldiers on a bridge over the Hu River. The Chinese successfully fought back this time. Four days later, Japan's prime minister, Prince Konoe, authorized Imperial troops to head from the home islands to China; at the same time, Chiang Kai-shek, China's Nationalist leader, mobilized his country's immense but ill-equipped two-million-man armies. Japan and China were now openly and brutally at war.

At first, Japan's forces steadily beat back the Chinese armies, quickly conquering Hankow and Canton and pillaging the Nationalist Chinese capital of Nanking. Stirred by belligerent media campaigns and propaganda, the Japanese at home strongly supported *seisen,* the "sacred war." "China news was everywhere," recalled machinist Kumagaya Tokuichi as the country expanded military production. By the end of 1937, he said, "Everybody in the country was working," and war, it seemed to him, was "not bad at all."

The following year, Japanese troops occupied most of China's fertile areas, but Japan's hold on the territory was insecure. Opposed by China's vast forces in a grueling war of attrition, the relatively small Japanese garrisons were unable to retain control of conquered areas. At the same time, international support for Japan was declining. In early 1939, the United States ended credit to Japan and imposed a "moral embargo" on the sale of airplanes and parts. The next year, America began embargoing the sale of aviation fuel, machine tools, and high-grade scrap metal. In response, conviction grew in Tokyo that Japan had to expand further to secure resources. In September 1940, Japanese forces moved into northern Indochina, and Japan signed the Tripartite Pact, forging an alliance with Germany and Italy against the United States and Europe's democracies.

Still, the China war ground on. More than a million Japanese soldiers were manning the garrisons in China by 1941, and millions of Chinese and some 300,000 Japanese troops had perished in the bitter conflict.

The "Shanghai Incident"

In March 1932, Japanese soldiers, *left,* advance cautiously through the ruins of the Chapei section of Shanghai in southern China. Incendiary bombs burned the residential area, leaving 250,000 Chinese residents homeless.

The Rape of Nanking

On December 14, 1937, Japanese soldiers, *right,* cheer after breaching the walls of Nanking, the capital of Nationalist China. Ordered to destroy the city, Japanese forces pillaged Nanking and nearby towns, raping thousands of women and massacring up to 300,000 people.

America's peacetime draft

In September 1940, Congress initiated the first peacetime military draft in U.S. history. On October 29, blindfolded Secretary of War Henry L. Stimson picked the first numbers to be called in the Selective Service lottery.

Fortress Hawaii

As tensions between the United States and Japan mounted, U.S. military leaders looked increasingly to America's mid-Pacific fortress island of Oahu, in the Hawaiian chain. Regarded as "the Gibraltar of the Pacific," in May 1940 Oahu was named the hub of the U.S. Pacific Fleet, which had previously been based in California. Now, in the shallow, sheltered waters of Pearl Harbor lay America's most powerful naval force under a single command: nine battleships, three aircraft carriers, twenty-one light and heavy cruisers, fifty-three destroyers, and twenty-three submarines—a show of battle strength, it was believed, that would help curb Japan's aggression in Southeast Asia and the Pacific. America had long recognized the military value of Hawaii, some twenty-four hundred miles west of California, but Pearl Harbor gained new strategic importance in the 1930s following Japan's invasion of Manchuria.

After the U.S. Pacific Fleet arrived in 1940 and military spending surged, thousands of construction workers shipped out to Oahu from the mainland to dredge Pearl Harbor and expand its dry-dock, power, and fuel storage facilities, equipping it to supply, shelter, and repair nearly all of the vessels in the American fleet. The $70 million naval installation at Pearl Harbor, protected by coral reefs and two mountain ranges, was also guarded by more than fourteen thousand army troops. With hundreds of army and navy planes and heavy artillery installations defending Pearl Harbor and the city of Honolulu, Oahu was considered virtually impregnable, "the strongest fortress in the world," in the words of General George C. Marshall, the United States Army Chief of Staff.

With its naval stronghold in the Pacific, "war with Japan," *Fortune* magazine stated in August 1940, "is the only war for which the U.S. is prepared." This assessment was overoptimistic, however, in the view of the U.S. fleet's commander in chief, Admiral James O. Richardson. The navy, Richardson knew, had many troubling vulnerabilities, including chronic shortages of ammunition, spare parts, and fuel. Richardson, moreover, believed that it was foolish to concentrate the fleet in Hawaiian waters. Hawaii was isolated in the Pacific, far from the West Coast yet dependent on the U.S. mainland for oil and other vital supplies. Its naval base at Pearl Harbor was America's only refueling, repair, and restocking point in the mid-Pacific—"a billion-dollar service station," some had called it—but it had a shortage of equipment for fueling ships at sea. In addition, Pearl Harbor's single,

Guarding the Pacific

U.S. warships began visiting the island of Oahu in the middle of the nineteenth century. In 1873, Generals John M. Schofield and B. S. Alexander surveyed Pearl Harbor, on the island's southern shore, and reported that it would make an ideal naval base.

narrow entrance, which required ships to enter and leave in single file, made it, Richardson said, "a God-damn mousetrap." On October 8, 1940, he straightforwardly told Roosevelt that "our fleet is disadvantageously disposed for preparing for or initiating war operations." Roosevelt responded to the criticism by removing Richardson from his command.

In February 1941, Admiral Husband E. Kimmel succeeded Richardson as commander of the U.S. Pacific Fleet. Like Richardson, Kimmel was aware of the navy's vulnerabilities in Hawaii. The fleet lacked personnel, and the admiral was especially concerned about aerial defenses: the army had an inadequate number of fighter and patrol planes, and many of those were obsolete. A few days after Kimmel relieved Richardson, Lieutenant General Walter C. Short arrived on Oahu to take up his new assignment as commander of the army's Hawaiian Department. Short, too, complained that Pearl Harbor had weak defenses against air raids. He also worried that the concentration of fighters and bombers at Wheeler and Hickam Fields, where they were parked in the open, exposed to possible attack, made them unusually difficult to protect. General Marshall

Change in command

Admiral Richardson, *above (right),* meets with navy officials in Washington, D.C., on October 10, 1940, to protest the concentration of U.S. naval power at Pearl Harbor. In February 1941, Richardson was replaced by Admiral Husband E. Kimmel, *left. Opposite,* an aerial view of Pearl Harbor, looking to the southwest, on October 30, 1941.

Sailing west for Hawaii

In April 1940, the U.S. Fleet sailed from California for the Navy's spring war games off Hawaii. The fleet then remained at Pearl Harbor instead of returning to its California base. In February 1941, President Roosevelt created separate Atlantic and Pacific Fleets, with the Pacific Fleet based permanently at Oahu. *Painting by C. S. Bailey.*

fully acknowledged the shortage of aircraft and anti-aircraft equipment at Pearl Harbor, but he was unable to remedy the situation, given America's overall military weakness. "We are tragically lacking in this matériel throughout the army," Marshall conceded, adding that "Hawaii is on a far better basis than any other command."

With responsibility for the army in Hawaii, Short's first duty was to protect the fleet. In the view of both Short and Marshall, this meant reducing the likelihood of sabotage—a key concern, given Hawaii's population of nearly 160,000 Hawaiian- and foreign-born Japanese. Beyond sabotage, however, Marshall instructed Short that, at Pearl Harbor, "a surprise raid by air and by submarine" constituted "the real perils of the situation." The potential for a surprise attack on Pearl Harbor had been openly acknowledged in the United States and Japan for years. Since 1931, in fact, every student at the Japanese military academy had faced a final-exam question on exactly how such an attack could be achieved. Pearl Harbor's vulnerability to a surprise raid was vividly demonstrated in February 1932, when U.S. Admiral Harry E. Yarnell, commanding the Carrier Battle Force during an exercise, successfully staged a mock surprise attack on the Hawaiian Islands at daybreak on a Sunday, targeting all the army aircraft and airfields. The Japanese, aware of this event, read reports describing the exercise in great detail. Washington, too, had long known "that a Japanese surprise attack on Pearl Harbor was always possible," according to Brigadier General Sherman Miles. In January 1941, Joseph Grew, the U.S. ambassador to Japan, even received information from Peru's minister to Tokyo that "Japanese military forces planned, in the event of trouble with the United States, to attempt a surprise mass attack on Pearl Harbor using all of their military facilities." The State Department, however, quickly dismissed the rumor, judging that an attack was highly unlikely, given the vast distances in the Pacific. As Commander

Island duty

Life on the balmy island of Oahu was "just fine," according to one marine, for servicemen who had "the price of a bus ticket and a beer or two."

Arsenal of democracy

While building up its naval presence in the Pacific, the United States was also producing quantities of arms and supplies to bolster Britain's war effort against Hitler through the Lend-Lease program, authorized by Congress in March 1941.

Vincent Murphy, Kimmel's assistant war plans officer, put it, "It would be utterly stupid for the Japanese to attack the United States at Pearl Harbor." American officials generally credited Japan's military leaders with having "the best of good sense."

By the spring of 1941, Americans were increasingly looking to the Atlantic as the probable theater of war. The United States was strengthening its commitment to Britain, providing it with "loaned" material and arms through the Lend-Lease program, which Congress authorized in March. With billions of dollars' worth of U.S. tanks, trucks, ammunition, planes, clothing, and food heading to beleaguered Britain, in exchange for "direct or indirect" payments instead of increasingly scarce cash, America was firmly establishing itself as an active, if noncombatant, enemy of the Axis powers. Although isolationists bitterly opposed Lend-Lease, other Americans believed that arming Britain—thus helping that country defeat Hitler—was the surest way for the United States to avoid entering the war.

At the same time, America's own military readiness continued to lag seriously. With much of the nation's military production diverted to Britain, equipment continued to be scarce. In May 1941, the United States Army had only one combat-ready division—compared to 208 for the Germans and more than 100 for the Japanese—and the U.S. Navy was just beginning to rebuild its strength. Heeding warnings that war with Japan would be "inevitable," Congress appropriated funds for a "two-ocean" navy in April 1940, but the expanded fleets remained "a strategic dream rather than a reality." Although the act was designed to triple the navy's size by 1944, no new keels were laid until 1941, and the fleet's full complement of ships was not expected to be ready until 1946 or 1947.

Given the weakness of America's armed forces and its increasing focus on events in Europe, Roosevelt believed that a war in the Pacific against Japan would be "the wrong war in the wrong ocean at the wrong time." With America ill-equipped to battle on two fronts, his strategy was to prepare for an Atlantic war against the Germans while stalling Japan, hoping that the presence of the Pacific Fleet would restrain it from further aggression.

To the Japanese, however, the powerful Pacific Fleet was not a deterrent, but rather "a dagger being pointed at our throat," Admiral Isoroku Yamamoto claimed. Anxious to gain control of crucial resources in Southeast Asia, the Japanese increasingly considered the possibility of neutralizing America's rising military threat and preparing for war with the United States. Japan had no illusions that it could defeat America's Hawaii-based fleet in a conventional sea battle. With the advantage of surprise, however, it might be able to strike a crushing blow.

In January 1941, Admiral Yamamoto actively began secret planning for a surprise, carrier-based air attack on Pearl Harbor's Pacific Fleet. There would be many problems to resolve, however, before Yamamoto's "Hawaii Operation" had any reasonable prospects of success. Most significant was the technical challenge of launching aerial torpedoes against ships in the shallow waters of the harbor, which were only about forty feet deep. Dropped from planes, aerial torpedoes would typically plunge to a depth of at least seventy-five feet before turning and hitting their targets; at Pearl Harbor, they would hit bottom before they had any chance to strike the U.S. ships. A second problem would be maintaining the critical element of surprise in an operation involving dozens of warships traveling vast distances across the Pacific. Finally, Yamamoto had to consider the risks of refueling warships at sea in the North Pacific Ocean, where weather conditions typically made that possible only seven days a month.

While Admiral Yamamoto assembled a planning team, Japan's government began seeking a diplomatic resolution to its growing tensions with the United States. Hoping to persuade the nation to relax its economic sanctions, the government dispatched Kichisaburo Nomura, a sixty-four-year-old retired admiral with little diplomatic experience, as its new ambassador to the United States. A political moderate, Nomura counted many Americans among his friends and opposed the bellicose policies of Japan's ultranationalist rulers. He believed there was "some slight chance of success in the negotiations"; those efforts, he hoped, "might be able to avoid a war in the Pacific." In March 1941, soon after arriving in Washington, Nomura began holding secret, informal diplomatic conversations with U.S. Secretary of State Cordell Hull, usually meeting clandestinely, without an interpreter, at Hull's Washington apartment.

Convinced that the Atlantic would be "the decisive theater" of engagement, navy officials dealt a serious blow to the U.S. Pacific Fleet in April and May 1941, when they transferred three of Kimmel's battleships, one aircraft carrier, seventeen destroyers, and four cruisers to the Atlantic Fleet. The move weakened by

Air power at sea

Admiral Isoroku Yamamoto, *right,* commander in chief of the combined fleet, was considered "the father of naval aviation" in Japan. For years, he had been convinced that air power held the key to future naval strategy, and he had spearheaded development of Japan's aircraft carrier fleet. In January 1941, Yamamoto began planning the "Hawaii Operation," a surprise aerial attack on Pearl Harbor, launched from a fleet of aircraft carriers. By the fall of 1941, Japan had built six carriers, including the *Kaga, below.* Together with destroyers, heavy cruisers, light cruisers, and other naval vessels, they formed the core of the Pearl Harbor striking force.

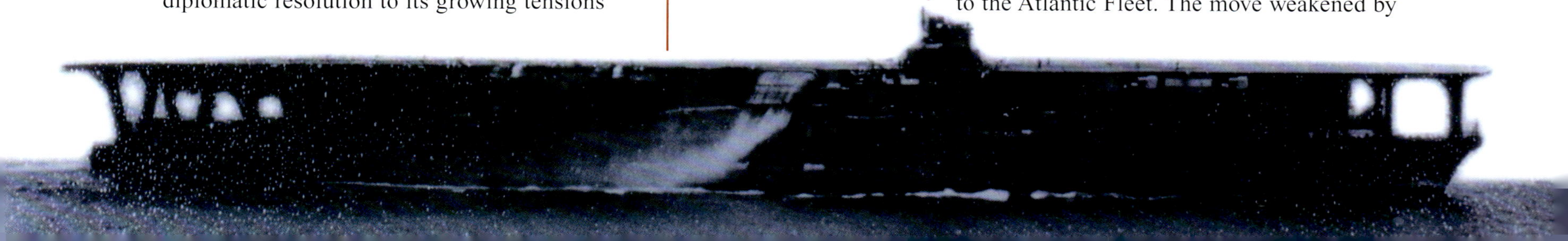

25 percent a Pacific naval force that was already, in Kimmel's estimation, "inferior to the Japanese Fleet in every category of fighting ship." Admiral Harold R. Stark, Chief of Naval Operations, had insisted on the transfer, anticipating Hitler's invasion of England; but instead, in June, Hitler suddenly turned east and attacked the Soviet Union. Germany's move prompted pledges of British and American military support for the Soviets, and it presented a potential new set of problems for Japan.

With less than a two-year supply of oil, Japan was under intensifying pressure to strike south. However, now that its ally Germany had invaded Russia, Japan's leaders debated whether to attack northward as well, invading Russian Siberia as Germany's partner. This strategy risked war not only with the Soviets but also with their new allies, the United States and Britain—a prospect that Japanese Prime Minister Fumimaro Konoe likened to "tackling the bear, the lion, and the eagle simultaneously, with side incursions into Indochina and the Netherlands East Indies, while still entwined in the dragon's tail." Rejecting this proposal, the Japanese government resolved instead to move quickly to expand its position in Southeast Asia, strengthening its future capacity to fight a global war. On July 14, Japan confronted the French government, demanding the right to occupy

Japan's envoys negotiate Admiral Kichisaburo Nomura *(seated at right)* and Saburo Kurusu were sent by Tokyo to negotiate with U.S. Secretary of State Cordell Hull in an effort to improve Japan's relations with America. At the same time, however, Japan was actively preparing for war with the United States in case diplomatic efforts failed.

southern Indochina. The French assented ten days later, and on July 28, forty thousand Japanese "peacefully" invaded Vietnam, Cambodia, and Laos, positioning Japan for further advances into British Malaya and Singapore, the Philippines, and the oil-rich Dutch East Indies.

This sudden deployment by Japan triggered a punishing American response. President Roosevelt had been well aware of the strategic debates leading up to Japan's latest incursion; in early 1941, the U.S. Army, in an operation known as "Magic," had cracked the secret Japanese diplomatic code, and Roosevelt had been able to follow Japan's Foreign Ministry communications. On July 25, he responded by freezing Japanese assets in the United States, a measure that effectively blocked all Japanese purchases of oil. Over the next two days, the British and Dutch joined America's economic blockade, shutting down 75 percent of Japan's international trade and cutting off 90 percent of its crucial oil supply.

Japan, thrown into deep crisis by the embargo, viewed the cooperation of the Americans, British, and Dutch as a mortal blow, an effort "to deny Japan her rightful place in the world by destroying her only available means of self-existence and self-defense." Convinced that America would oppose further territorial advances with force and compel her withdrawal from China, Japan decided to strike first before the United States military was fully mobilized. At an Imperial war conference on September 6, Japan's leaders agreed to prepare for war with the United States. Still, however, they would press on with negotiations. If Japan could persuade America to end the embargo and its aid to China, war might yet be avoided. Japan's position hardened in October when General Hideki Tojo replaced Konoe as prime minister and minister of war. Tojo, blunt and aggressive, was former chief of staff of the Kwantung army in Manchuria. Known as *kamisori* (razor blade), he argued that Japan should be ready to go to war with America in early December. If diplomatic efforts had not been fruitful by that time, political and military leaders agreed, Japan would launch a strike against the United States.

In November, to spearhead the last, crucial round of negotiations, Tokyo sent a seasoned envoy, Saburo Kurusu, to join Nomura in Washington. Nomura and Hull had been continuing their diplomatic conversations since March, but without any significant results. Nevertheless, the United States, like Japan, viewed these talks as an important opportunity to avoid war in the Pacific. America was in the midst of rearming while providing aid to its allies in Europe. If negotiators could stall Japan until 1942, the country would be better prepared to wage war on two fronts.

Prime Minister Tojo

In July 1940, General Hideki Tojo joined the cabinet of Japanese Prime Minister Prince Konoe as minister of war. Intensely anti-Western and anti-Communist, Tojo was a veteran of Japanese forces in Manchuria and advocated Japan's aggressive military and economic domination of East Asia. He succeeded Konoe as prime minister in October 1941, while simultaneously functioning as home minister and minister of war. A leader of the militarist faction, he determined, on December 1, 1940, that Japan "could not achieve [its] goals by means of diplomacy."

Breaking the Japanese Code

On September 10, 1940, a twenty-six-year-old U.S. Army cryptanalyst named Genevieve Grotjan was studying a coded Japanese message in the Munitions Building in Washington, D.C. Suddenly, she saw a pattern among the characters she was analyzing. Within minutes, her colleagues on the army's codebreaking team realized what Grotjan had accomplished—she had unlocked the secret of a vital Japanese encryption system known as Purple.

The Purple system coded diplomatic messages sent between Japan's foreign ministry and all of its embassies abroad. It was one of several Japanese encryption systems that were collectively known in the United States as Magic. The Japanese diplomatic cables were intercepted at army and navy listening posts in the United States and many of its territories, including Bainbridge Island, Washington; Panama; Cavite, the Philippines; and San Francisco. Once messages were detected, they were sent on to army and navy intelligence sections for decoding. The relay process could be extremely slow. San Francisco and Bainbridge Island were the only stations with teletype facilities. Other interception posts dispatched the coded messages to army and navy intelligence in Washington, D.C., using ship, train, or weekly airmail.

To keep Japan from learning that the United States had cracked its diplomatic codes, only a few officials in Washington were permitted to see the decoded and translated messages, including the president, the secretary of war, the secretary of the navy, the chief of naval operations, and the directors of naval and military intelligence. On the other hand, Japan's military codes had not been cracked, and as a result, American analysts were not privy to details of Japanese army and navy preparations.

In the torrent of Magic diplomatic intercepts, however, experts were able to glean some crucial military information. Thanks to Magic, in July 1941 President Roosevelt gained full knowledge of Japan's "peaceful" invasion plans for southern Indochina. Still, because Japan's military leaders maintained strict secrecy about the planned Pearl Harbor operation, even within the ranks of their own government, decoded diplomatic messages provided little or no warning of the attack.

Deciphering machines

Once the Purple coding system was broken, U.S. experts constructed elaborate decryption machines that were sent to priority locations. Seven Purple machines had been completed by mid-1941. Four were in Washington, D.C., two were in Great Britain, and one had been dispatched to U.S. naval forces in the Philippines. No Purple machine was supplied to the army and navy commanders at Pearl Harbor.

Before Kurusu and Nomura began their final round of talks in mid-November, the Americans already knew of Japan's negotiating positions and deadline from deciphered diplomatic messages. The negotiators were considering a range of stopgap proposals, but, as the month wore on, Secretary of State Hull became increasingly reluctant to accept these partial measures, having gleaned from decoded messages that Japan was readying its military for further strikes at targets that had not yet been revealed.

Finally, on November 26, Hull flatly rejected Japan's negotiating offers and presented America's demand for its total withdrawal of all forces from China and Indochina. The U.S. position, in effect, would return Japan to its territorial status of the 1920s. Kurusu, replying to Hull, conceded that now he "did not see how any agreement was possible." America's position, he declared, was "tantamount to meaning the end."

Following that confrontation, the army and navy dispatched "war warnings" to the Philippines, Hawaii, and other commands, alerting U.S. forces to expect an "aggressive move" by the Japanese. The location of Japan's strike was expected to be in Southeast Asia—the Philippines, Thailand, Borneo, or the Malay Peninsula. No mention whatever was made of a possible attack on the Hawaiian Islands. Admiral Kimmel, receiving this warning in Pearl Harbor, ordered the Pacific Fleet to exercise extreme vigilance against submarines operating in the area. He did not, however, order aerial patrols to protect the fleet against a possible surprise attack.

Diplomatic stalemate

Japan's envoy Kichisaburo Nomura *(far left)* strolls near the White House with U.S. Secretary of State Cordell Hull and Saburo Kurusu during their difficult and unsuccessful diplomatic talks.

Defending Pearl Harbor

On February 4, 1941, Lieutenant General Walter C. Short, *below,* assumed command of the Hawaiian Department of the Army. It was the army's responsibility to defend the warships in Pearl Harbor and the coastline of the Hawaiian Islands against attack. Short's most pressing concerns, however, were training thousands of raw recruits and protecting army bases against the possibility of local sabotage.

Owing to equipment shortages, he had only forty-nine patrol planes available in flying condition, instead of the 250 he believed he needed for effective, 360-degree patrols against an air attack. Kimmel declined to order partial patrols.

Lieutenant General Walter C. Short also received a war warning informing him that "hostile action" by the Japanese was "possible at any moment." The alert instructed Short to "undertake . . . reconnaissance and other measures . . . so as not, repeat not, to alarm civil population or disclose intent." Short responded to these orders by simply putting his forces on a low-level alert to prevent sabotage, since, he believed, "air attack was not imminent" and "sabotage was our gravest danger," given Hawaii's large population of Japanese. To guard the army's aircraft more effectively, he ordered all planes disarmed and parked closely together in the airfields. In addition, Short ordered all anti-aircraft ammunition carefully locked away so that it would not fall into the hands of saboteurs.

Some three thousand miles to the northwest, Japanese warships were already sailing into the rough waters of the North Pacific, under strict radio silence. Since September 1941, special flight crews of the Imperial Navy's First Air Fleet

had been drilling intensively, practicing stuntlike bombing maneuvers with no knowledge of their mission.

By the end of the summer, they had honed techniques of horizontal bombing to neutralize anti-aircraft fire, and in November the problem of aerial torpedoing in shallow waters was solved. Japanese military planners by that time had also assembled detailed information about army and navy installations and routines at Pearl Harbor.

Since April, they had been receiving clandestine reports from a naval reserve ensign named Takeo Yoshikawa, who secretly scouted Oahu's bases while assigned to the Japanese Consulate in Honolulu. Exploring the island by taxi and chauffeured car, Yoshikawa regularly visited a teahouse in the Alewa Heights hills above Pearl Harbor, where he carefully observed naval activity with the help of a telescope available to its customers.

Training for attack

For three months before the Pearl Harbor raid, Japanese naval aviators trained rigorously, with no information about the surprise attack. Crews practiced bombing battleship-size targets and honed techniques for torpedo-bombing in shallow water. Japanese fighter pilots were already well seasoned from their combat missions in the China war. "Every pilot was confident of his plane," recalled Commander Minoru Genda. Because of limited launch space on the carriers, the aerial attack was divided into two successive waves, each led by expert, hand-picked fliers.

Other observation posts gave him clear views of Pearl Harbor's submarine base and Ford Island in the center of the harbor. Over time, Yoshikawa discovered that most of the ships in the Pacific Fleet were moored in Pearl Harbor on weekends and that Oahu's air patrols routinely ignored the island's northern sector. He forwarded all of this detailed information to Japan.

By the beginning of November 1941, the combined fleet of the Japanese Navy was training seven days a week for the attack, and Japan's leaders had finalized war plans. Only a breakthrough in negotiations could stop the accelerating preparations for war. On November 17, the flagship carrier *Akagi* stealthily left Japan for remote Hitokappu Bay in the Kurile Islands, off the south coast of Kamchatka. Over the next five days, traveling one by one and taking separate routes to avoid detection, a massive strike force of Japanese carriers, battleships, heavy and light cruisers, destroyers, submarines, and tankers assembled at that cold, isolated outpost, awaiting their departure orders for Pearl Harbor.

There, the mission was finally revealed to the crew. Each day from then on, the pilots studied a precise, six-foot model of Oahu that was kept aboard the *Akagi*, carefully memorizing their individual approach routes and the actions they would take during the attack. Then, on the dark, cloudy morning of November 26,

World War II Japanese military flight helmet

the thirty-ship task force, commanded by Vice Admiral Chuichi Nagumo, secretly weighed anchor and sailed out in heavy winds into the North Pacific, heading eastward toward the Aleutians and Midway Island. Loaded with fuel, with oil drums packed into the living quarters, the task force traveled in formation—carriers in parallel columns of three, followed by tankers, flanked by battleships and heavy cruisers, and encircled by a screen of light cruisers and destroyers. Some two hundred miles ahead, the Japanese submarines patrolled the seas. If an enemy fleet was spotted at any time up until two days before the attack, the strike force had instructions to reverse course and immediately abandon the operation. To maintain secrecy, no trash was thrown overboard, all transmitters were sealed, and blackouts were carefully maintained; at night, each ship followed only the white wake of the vessel ahead of it.

Assembling the force

By November 22, the entire Japanese strike force had gathered at Hitokappu Bay on the island of Etorofu in the Kuriles. The location was selected for secrecy as well as its remote northern location. Four days later, the attack force left the Kuriles, heading due east across the north Pacific.

In Japan, the decision for war had been confirmed. Tokyo had received the Hull note on November 27, stunning Japan's leaders. Four days later, on December 1, they gathered at an Imperial conference, declaring that negotiations with the United States had been futile. "Our nation . . . stands at a crossroad," Tojo stated, "one leading to glory and the other to decline." Although he was "loath to compel our people to suffer even greater hardships," there was now

Remote route

The Japanese carrier force followed the northern route to Hawaii because few ships navigated that part of the Pacific Ocean in winter. The strike force had orders to abandon the Pearl Harbor operation if it was discovered before reaching the designated launch point for the attack. Here, the *Kaga,* on the horizon, is followed by the carrier *Zuikaku.*

no time to lose. The ratio of armaments between Japan and the United States, especially air power, would only become more unfavorable to Japan in time. "Under the circumstances," Tojo announced, "our Empire has no alternative but to begin war against the United States . . . in order to resolve the present crisis and assure survival." If Japan was going to strike, it would have to do so quickly. As Tojo once remarked, "sometimes a man has to jump with his eyes closed from the temple of Kiyomizu into the ravine below."

Out in the Pacific, the Japanese strike force sailed steadily east from the Kuriles, in a cold wind and a quiet sea. The young men of the carrier flight crews, filled with fighting spirit, steeled themselves for their coming mission. "Hard nights and days of training had been followed by hasty preparations," remembered Captain Mitsuo Fuchida, who was aboard the flagship *Akagi*. Now, on the sortie, each man at last knew that he was going to war. From the Kuriles, the young fliers and crew members had written and sent home their final letters; most, recalled Lieutenant Commander Sadao Chigusa, were last wills and testaments, written "assuming that we would not come back alive."

Carrier deck

On Admiral Nagumo's flagship carrier *Akagi, right,* planes wait on the flight deck as the vessel steams toward the launch point in the Pacific.

Takeoff

Crew members, *below,* wave their caps as a torpedo bomber speeds down the *Akagi*'s deck.

Hawaii: Gibraltar of the Pacific

"Decades of advertising and movie iteration have convinced practically every stranger outside the islands that Hawaii is still a semi-civilized Eden where heavy-bodied, sleepy-eyed Polynesian girls go about in ti-leaf skirts and do the hula. . . . [But] Hawaii—or the island of Oahu—is first of all a fort . . . [that] gives us a long jump on the Japanese when and if the great Pacific War of the future breaks out."
—*Fortune,* August 1940

Second Lieutenant Revella Guest, an army nurse from the state of Maine, was transferred to Oahu in March 1941 and found herself suddenly in an island post that was "beautiful . . . exciting . . . gorgeous."

Navy Painter Third Class Henry Retzloff Jr., who hailed from Michigan, enjoyed his new life in Hawaii, too—girls, beaches, lots of liberty, and a workload that was rarely too demanding.

Hawaii, before the Second World War, was crowded with American servicemen and women

Troops in paradise

Even as early as 1898, soldiers in the American garrison on Oahu enjoyed the tropical pleasures that Honolulu offered troops: free haircuts and streetcar rides, roast chicken and potato salad luau feasts, and complimentary doughnuts and coffee from the Red Cross. By 1941, however, island life was not only about tropical temptations such as hula lessons, surfing, swimming, and beach parties. Some soldiers complained of boredom, there were housing shortages, and Honolulu prices were soaring. The cost of a pint of milk had doubled to ten cents, and restaurants were charging the then-exorbitant price of thirty cents for a couple of scrambled eggs.

who had been shipped out to the islands to fortify Oahu's fast-expanding army and navy bases. Ever since 1898, when America transported large numbers of troops to the Philippines during the Spanish-American War, the United States had recognized the military importance of Hawaii. Located some twenty-four hundred miles west of California and thirty-four hundred miles east of Japan, the Hawaiian island chain served as a strategic sentinel in the middle of the Pacific Ocean. "No enemy could approach the mainland without leaving its flank exposed," a journalist judged in 1936, and no enemy would be able to "pause to engage Hawaii, to overwhelm it, without the expenditure of much time and energy."

Since 1778, when British Captain James Cook first visited the islands, the Polynesian kingdom of Hawaii had lured an international population attracted to its whaling and sandalwood trades. In 1898 the United States annexed Hawaii, and that year the first permanent American garrison settled in at Camp McKinley near Diamond Head, the extinct volcano that rises over Honolulu's southeast shore.

Oahu's expansive naval basin of Pearl Harbor was originally used by the American navy as a coaling station during the Spanish-American War. Discovered by westerners

August 1940 issue of Fortune

in 1793, the harbor, originally called *Wai momi* (water of pearl), had been used by the Hawaiians for fishponds and pearl-bearing oysters. In 1816, when Russian explorer Otto Von Kotzbue visited the site, he predicted that it could one day be the finest harbor in the world. However, with its mouth blocked by a coral reef and sandbar, permitting only ships with a fifteen-foot draft to enter, the harbor remained undeveloped and undredged until after annexation.

On May 1, 1908, Congress authorized the construction of the Pearl Harbor Naval Shipyard to provide repair and dry-dock facilities for American warships in the Pacific. When military aviation took off after the First World War, airfields were established on Ford Island in the center of Pearl Harbor and, in later years, at Wheeler, Hickam, and Bellows Fields.

By 1940, following Japan's aggression in China and the outbreak of war in Europe, Hawaii gained new strategic importance for the United States. That year, the navy's fleet exercises were held in Hawaiian waters, and hundreds of millions of dollars were appropriated for military construction on Oahu. Thousands of civilians were recruited from the mainland to work at the fast-expanding Pearl Harbor navy yard, and military facilities were rapidly improved. On February 1, 1941, Pearl Harbor was named the permanent base of the U.S. Pacific Fleet. By then, Hawaii was "reputed to be

Leis and luaus
Between the wars, many American servicemen in Hawaii, like these sailors at a local luau, made the most of island hospitality.

the most intensively fortified area under the American flag," according to *Foreign Policy Reports*, ". . . and is probably the strongest outlying base of any nation in the world." With big guns defending the Pacific Fleet at Forts Weaver, Kamehameha, Shafter, and Barrette; extensive ammunition depots; heavy artillery defenses around Honolulu at Fort DeRussy and at Fort Ruger atop Diamond Head; mule trails, roads, and railways; fleet personnel totaling around seventy thousand; and some twenty-five thousand army troops, Oahu dominated the mid-Pacific as, one expert observed, "a tacit if not fully effective barrier to Japan's southward advance in Asia."

Hawaii's civilian population was also well prepared for the possibility of war. Honolulu's city and county governments had devised a comprehensive emergency disaster plan, and a Major Disaster Council, with thousands of volunteers, was poised to take charge of civilian activities in war. The Red Cross held first-aid classes, a blood plasma bank was established, plans were in place to convert schools into hospitals, and Honolulu residents held "blackout parties" during civilian defense drills. In October 1941, Hawaii's legislature passed the Hawaii Defense Act, empowering the territory's governor, Joseph Poindexter, to respond effectively to any emergency conditions.

Food supply was an important consideration. Hawaii's agricultural economy was based on the production of sugar and pineapples, industries that employed 65 percent of the local labor force. As a result, Oahu produced only 15 percent of its food and imported more than 60 percent of its supplies from the American mainland. In the event of war, U.S. Army plans called for converting all of the sugar and pineapple acreage to other food crops, a prospect the local growers did not relish. As one writer observed, Hawaii's powerful plantation owners "like their island paradise—and are praying that the great Pacific War is still a Sunday supplement's bad dream."

Sweet liberty

Many sailors on shore leave on Oahu headed straight for the Black Cat bar in downtown Honolulu. Other popular spots for seamen on liberty included watering holes like the New Senator Hotel. "We felt rather secure in our enjoyment of the pleasures offered in this piece of paradise," one navy officer remembered, "so safely isolated on this broad expanse of the Pacific Ocean." *Below left,* sailor leans against a surfboard.

Rising sun over Oahu

Sunrise at Pearl Harbor "was itself a religious experience," recalled John Rampley, a crew member on the *Arizona*. "With the stillness and quietness which surrounded the water," it was as if every dawn was "an Easter sunrise service."

DECEMBER '41

Grim and intent, President Roosevelt, increasingly worried about the prospect of war with the Japanese, raced back to Washington from Warm Springs, Georgia, where he had celebrated a brief Thanksgiving holiday. Returning early to the capital on December 1 aboard a special train, the president arrived at the White House shortly before noon and met immediately with Secretary of State Hull, who had just spent more than an hour speaking with Kurusu and Nomura. The two Japanese envoys had emerged from that discussion somber-faced but still insisting that the United States and Japan had not yet reached "the end of the talks."

Nevertheless, the possibility of war with Japan now loomed more threateningly than ever. Negotiations, for all intents and purposes, had stalled. Tokyo had not yet formally replied to Hull's November 26 demands; meanwhile, reports were coming in that Japan was massing its forces menacingly in Southeast Asia.

Japanese national flag

A Japanese attack on British possessions in Asia might be the trigger that would bring America to the brink of war. At a luncheon on December 1, Roosevelt privately assured Lord Halifax, Britain's ambassador to Washington, that in the case of such an assault, "then, of course, we will be in it together." Despite the warning signs and rising alarm, however, it was still unclear when and where the Japanese would strike. "It is all in the laps of the gods," Roosevelt admitted that day to Treasury Secretary Henry Morgenthau.

Army and navy intelligence experts were continuing to intercept top-secret Japanese diplomatic messages. But, despite the impressive capabilities of Magic and the Purple deciphering machine, U.S. monitors had inexplicably lost track of ten of Japan's aircraft carriers, warships that had been mysteriously "missing" now for several weeks. On November 14, American military analysts had speculated that the ships were probably still in Japan's home waters. Owing in part to the strict radio silence observed by the Japanese Combined Fleet—now secretly speeding toward Hawaii—American monitors had no reliable clues as to the carriers' location. This was not an unusual lapse in American intelligence gathering. Between June and December 1941, there were more than fifty days when Americans were unable to locate Japan's battleships, and more than eighty days when most cruisers in Japan's First Fleet were "missing." Even the Japanese carrier fleet itself had somehow "disappeared" for 134 days during that period.

Ships in harbor

A sailor poses by a five-inch anti-aircraft gun on the deck of the battleship *Arizona*. In December 1941, the *Arizona* was one of nine battleships in the U.S. Pacific Fleet. One of them, the *Colorado*, was undergoing repairs on the West Coast. All of the other ships were in Pearl Harbor.

Acknowledging this situation, Kimmel's fleet intelligence officer, Lieutenant Commander Edwin T. Layton, admitted to the admiral on December 2 that he had "almost a complete blank of information on the carriers today." Kimmel somewhat jokingly asked Layton, "Do you mean to say that they could be rounding Diamond Head and you wouldn't know it?" Layton replied, "I hope they would be sighted before now." Kimmel and his staff were not only in the dark about the location of the Japanese carriers; they were also unaware of several curious Japanese messages that analysts in Washington had intercepted. In particular, one decoded dispatch translated on October 9 amounted, in essence, to "a bombing plan for Pearl Harbor": a request from Tokyo that the Japanese consul in Honolulu provide detailed information on the positions of all ships moored at the Hawaiian base. The contents of this message were never relayed to Kimmel. The admiral, in fact, had so little information from intelligence that he did not know what a Purple decoding machine was until the first week in December. None of the devices had ever been dispatched to Hawaii.

Although the Pacific Fleet

Coastal defense

Situated at Diamond Head, *left,* the extinct volcano overlooking Honolulu, the army's big guns at Fort Ruger protected the entrance to the city's harbor. Other heavy artillery installations guarded the Oahu coastline from Forts DeRussy and Armstrong at Honolulu to Forts Weaver, Kamehameha, and Barrette near Pearl Harbor.

On the town

Sightseeing sailors, *far left,* pose by the statue of King Kamehameha I outside the Hawaii Judiciary Building in Honolulu. During the reign of Kamehameha the Great in the early 1800s, the kingdom of Hawaii became an important center of international trade in the Pacific.

had received numerous warnings of possible aggression by Japan, not one of these alerts had pointed to a potential air raid on Pearl Harbor. Instead, indications as late as December 1 specified a possible Japanese move against Thailand's Isthmus of Kra, which controlled access to Malaya, the Dutch East Indies, and Burma. Kimmel and Short, confident that Japan posed no direct threat to the Oahu base, focused not on defense preparations but on the ongoing task of training thousands of raw recruits for war. Although the army and navy in Hawaii had prepared a joint plan to protect the islands from attack, the two services in reality knew little about each other's capabilities. According to the plan, the navy would be responsible for long-range air patrols to detect enemy forces, while the army would fight off an aerial attack with fighter planes and anti-aircraft guns. There was so little communication and coordination, however, that Short's chief of staff, Colonel Walter Phillips, conceded that he "never knew what the navy had" in regard to the number and capabilities of patrol planes. And, despite their regular golf dates every other Sunday at Fort Shafter, Kimmel and Short never discussed army and navy aerial defense. As Short remarked later, "Neither of us would have wanted the other to be prying into matters that didn't concern him."

Pearl Harbor's defensive capabilities were declining by the first week of December. With two aircraft carrier groups at sea, carrying dozens of navy and marine fighter planes, the fleet's long-range scouting abilities were

6S14
6S2

handicapped. On November 28, a task force with the carrier *Enterprise* had left Pearl Harbor for Wake Island under Vice Admiral William F. Halsey's command, and on December 5, a second task force with the carrier *Lexington* departed for Midway under Rear Admiral John H. Newton. Although both carriers were conducting routine air patrols of a vast, five-thousand-mile swath of the Pacific west of Oahu, scanning the seas between Midway, Wake, Pearl Harbor, and Johnston Island, the ocean north of Oahu was not patrolled. Many of the aircraft still on the island had only arrived in November and had not yet been checked out and equipped to fly. Meanwhile, Rear Admiral Claude Bloch, commandant of the Fourteenth Naval District, was so worried about the lack of spare parts for the PBY patrol planes remaining on Oahu that he did not want to "fritter" any of them away in distant reconnaissance efforts. The navy did continue to send planes out on regular training patrols north of Oahu, scouting distances as great as four hundred miles. These northern patrol flights, however, were halted on Thursday, December 4, and the planes were subsequently ordered to remain on the ground for maintenance.

In addition to the shortage of parts and patrol planes, the sortie of the fast carrier groups, with their escorts of swift destroyers and heavy cruisers, had left the fleet's slow battleships in port without air cover in case of an enemy attack. For the first time since July 4, all of the Pacific Fleet's eight battleships were moored or anchored in Pearl Harbor together, an unusual event. Kimmel now faced the decision of whether to keep the warships in port—where they could be a tempting target—or send them out to sea on a sortie. His staff argued persuasively that the battleships should remain at Pearl. Without the air cover provided by the carriers, it could be dangerous to send the ships out in an area likely to be crawling with Japanese submarines. In the shallow waters of Pearl Harbor, however, the ships should not only be safe from a torpedo-plane attack, but they would also have had the added protection of the army's planes and anti-aircraft guns. Tight fuel supplies also factored into the decision. Ships at sea burned a lot of oil. To keep the fleet out and exhaust Pearl Harbor's fuel reserves, "only to find that such expenditures were unnecessary or, still worse, to have the entire fleet short of fuel when action was joined," Kimmel reasoned, seemed a foolish choice to make, based merely on "indefinite information or conjecture." Finally, the admiral's staff argued that an emergency order canceling shore leaves and sending the fleet to sea would

Carrier task forces

A squadron of SBD dive bombers, *left,* soars above the aircraft carrier *Enterprise,* stationed at Pearl Harbor. All three carriers in the Pacific Fleet were out of the harbor on December 7, 1941. On November 28, the *Enterprise* left Pearl Harbor for Wake Island, with three heavy cruisers and nine destroyers, in a task force commanded by Vice Admiral Halsey. On December 5, the aircraft carrier *Lexington* sortied with three heavy cruisers and five destroyers. Commanded by Rear Admiral Newton, the *Lexington* task force sailed for Midway Island. The third aircraft carrier based at Pearl Harbor, the *Saratoga,* was in San Diego.

Calm before the storm

Servicemen, *right,* savor simple pleasures of Hawaiian life before Japan's attack.

attract far too much public attention. Weighing all of these considerations, Kimmel determined to keep the battleships in port.

Orders were issued to the based fleet to prepare for an Admiral's Inspection after the weekend. Complying with these orders, crews on many ships removed all live ammunition from ready boxes kept near anti-aircraft guns and padlocked it securely in the magazines below. They took apart and stowed the guns' firing locks. In addition, waiving navy regulations requiring all watertight compartments to be closed in port, crews were ordered to open all hatches to air out watertight compartments—a risky move, since it compromised the ships' ability to survive flooding. Inspection orders also called for opening the shock-absorbing, watertight "blisters" that ran along the length of many ships, compartments designed to reduce the impact of torpedoes and minimize their damage to the ship's interior.

Wheeler Field

Ground crews position a P-36 fighter plane at Wheeler Field, an air base in the center of Oahu. Wheeler was home to most of the combat aircraft on the island. On November 27, Lieutenant General Short ordered all planes at Wheeler removed from their protective bunkers and parked wing to wing out in the open, so that they could easily be guarded against the threat of sabotage.

On the ground, too, as a result of the army's sabotage alert, live ammunition stores were locked away. Under these conditions, it would take hours to prepare the army's large-caliber anti-aircraft guns—the fleet's major defense—for firing. Short, like Kimmel, was eager to avoid creating any kind of panic on the island, especially given the instructions from Washington "not . . . to alarm civilian population or disclose intent." As a result, he had chosen to activate the lowest-level sabotage alert, believing that it would not be noticed by the island residents. In accordance with this alert, most of the army's pursuit planes—the only fighters that were modern enough to combat an aerial attack—were parked wing-to-wing, unarmed and unfueled, in Oahu's airfields. The army was also in the midst of remodeling its battle command center, and switchboards and other key equipment were disconnected. Other rapid communications links were safely locked up to avoid sabotage.

At the same time, life in Hawaii for civilians and many in the military was jammed with the pleasant distractions of the season. Army flying crews at Wheeler Field looked forward to Christmastime beach picnics and beer parties, and the circus was coming to Schofield Barracks. Sailors and troops were invited to potluck suppers, band concerts, and musical shows, such as *Down Town Frolics* and a revue by the Hickam High Hatters. There were also movies playing at theaters around Honolulu: *Only Angels Have Wings,* starring Rita Hayworth, and Bob Hope's 1939 release, *Never Say Die.*

Although the local papers warned of an impending crisis with Japan, the mood on Oahu was, for the most part, blithely unconcerned with coming danger. "Scuttlebutt was," said George Waller, a gunner's mate on the battleship *Maryland,* that the Japanese "would never attack Pearl because they just didn't have enough to do it. If they did, however, they wouldn't last three weeks because we could beat them in that time." Not everyone, however, felt quite so confident. On Sunday, November 30, a front-page, banner headline in the *Honolulu Advertiser* warned: "JAPANESE MAY STRIKE OVER THE WEEKEND!" The warning put navy wife Celia R. Illum on edge. If the article was accurate, she imagined, the Japanese "could have a field day out here with all those ships lined up." Her husband, Frank, an ensign on the minelayer *Oglala,* dismissed her worries. "That could never happen," he assured her; "we'd know miles out before they could get near Pearl Harbor."

Despite the newspaper warnings, army troops and navy crew members simply got on with their ordinary duties. "Those days were every-days in my life. It was routine," remembered Seaman First Class Nick L. Kouretas, a crew member on the light cruiser *Raleigh.* On Friday, December 5, some of the men on the *Arizona* came on board the battleship *Nevada* to watch a movie—*One Foot in Heaven,* remembered Dan Wentreck, a fireman

Servicewomen on Oahu

Military women as well as men shipped out to Pearl Harbor before the war. In December 1941, scores of army and navy nurses were serving in medical facilities on Oahu's bases. "It was nice living," remembered Second Lieutenant Ada M. Olsson, who was stationed at Schofield Barracks Army Hospital and spent much of her free time at the beach.

Aloha spirit

Sailors serenade a sunbather on the beach at Waikiki in Honolulu.

from the *Nevada.* On the next day, Saturday, December 6, holiday routine was declared, and many of the enlisted men and officers went out on liberty. Their attitude, Wentreck recalled, was, "Happy days are here again." On the national scene, too, the gravity of international tensions was offset by unshakable confidence. Secretary of the Navy Frank Knox boasted in *American* magazine that with "the greatest navy in the world," America was prepared to meet any emergency in the Atlantic or Pacific, or in both oceans at once. Maine's Republican senator, Ralph Owen Brewster, declared on a visit to Puerto Rico that "the United States Navy can defeat the Japanese Navy any place and at any time."

Trouble ahead

Frank Knox—holding binoculars, with Marines on joint maneuvers—served as Secretary of the Navy under Franklin Roosevelt from 1940 to 1944. On December 5, 1941, Knox reported to President Roosevelt that "he thought the Japanese were up to something."

Officials in Washington were steeling themselves for a Japanese attack somewhere far across the globe in Asia. At the president's December 5 cabinet meeting, "there was never a flicker of an idea expressed by anybody that the Japanese might at the time engage in war with the United States," recalled Secretary of Labor Frances Perkins. "Instead," she said, "the discussion involved how we thought the Japanese would go about attacking the British, who had done nothing to the Japanese but did hold Singapore, which was presumed to be the key to Asiatic control." At the meeting, Secretary Knox reported that the navy now knew for a fact that the Japanese fleet was out at sea. Although he admitted that his information was not perfect, there was every indication, he said, that they were going south toward Singapore. He noted that within the next week they would have a firmer indication of where the fleet was going. As cabinet members left the meeting, Perkins recalled, "I suppose everybody felt the same way, that we had a dreadful, dreadful situation. I remember going back to my office and just sitting down kind of limp, trying to face the music. It was a very shattering day, but there was still no sense of anything immediate."

Knox's information was confirmed the next morning. At 10:40 A.M. on Saturday, December 6, the State Department learned that two large parties of Japanese transports, cruisers, and destroyers had been seen sailing west from Cambodia to the Isthmus of Kra. Meeting with the navy's senior staff to discuss the Japanese fleet movements, Knox asked, "Gentlemen, are they going to hit us?" Rear Admiral Richmond Kelly Turner replied, "No, Mr. Secretary. They are going to attack the British. They are not ready for us yet." No one at the meeting disagreed.

Even with Britain as Japan's likely target, it was clear to many that conditions were approaching a crisis. Secretary of War Henry L. Stimson changed his plans for the weekend so that he could be easily reached if necessary. At the White House that afternoon, hoping to stave off a confrontation with Japan, President Roosevelt composed a direct, personal appeal in a letter to Emperor Hirohito. "During the past few weeks," the president wrote, "it has become clear to the world that Japanese military, naval, and air forces have been sent to Southern Indo-China in such large numbers as to create a reasonable doubt . . . that this continuing concentration . . . is not defensive in its character. . . . A continuance of such a situation is unthinkable. . . . A withdrawal of the Japanese forces from Indo-China would result in the assurance of peace throughout the whole of the South Pacific area. . . . I am confident that both of us . . . have a sacred duty to restore traditional amity and prevent further death and destruction in the world."

As soon as he finished the letter, Roosevelt cabled it in code to the U.S. Embassy in Tokyo for delivery to the emperor through America's ambassador, Joseph Grew. Because the message was sent in code, however, a military censor in Tokyo, following routine procedure, delayed Roosevelt's message for ten hours. That night, Admiral Stark's aide, Lieutenant Commander William R. Smedberg III, worked late, until 7:00 or 8:00 P.M., "but there was no great excitement," he recalled. "Through our intelligence, we had been watching the Japanese warships and transports that were headed for the Isthmus of Kra. . . . As we left the office, one of us said, 'Well, the

Emperor of Japan

Emperor Hirohito ruled Japan for sixty-three years in a reign known as *Showa*, or "Enlightened Peace." Although he knew that Japan's expansionist policies could ignite war with Britain and the United States, Hirohito approved moving Japanese troops into southern Indochina. Beginning in early November 1941, he was fully informed about plans for the Pearl Harbor attack.

Carrier power in the Pacific

The aircraft carrier *Lexington* sails past Waikiki in the early 1930s. In February 1932, the *Lexington* took part in joint army-navy war games in which the U.S. fleet simulated a carrier air attack on army and air corps bases in Hawaii. During the mock raid, staged at daybreak on a Sunday, U.S. carrier aircraft attacked Oahu in two waves, taking all their targets by surprise and demonstrating the offensive power of carrier aviation. Japan's attack on Pearl Harbor, nearly ten years later, "was almost a perfect duplicate," remembered Admiral Arthur W. Radford, who took part in the exercise as an aide to the aircraft battle force commander.

British are sure going to catch it tomorrow at Singapore.' We didn't have the slightest suspicion that there was any threat to Pearl Harbor."

Meanwhile, the Foreign Ministry in Tokyo was preparing to transmit its long-awaited reply to the Hull note, a lengthy message that Japan wanted to present to the Americans on Sunday. The text of the message, made up of seven sections, was being transmitted from Tokyo in fourteen separate telegrams to Japan's embassy in Washington. There, the staff was instructed to decode it, translate it from Japanese to English, and type it up without the assistance of American clerks. Tokyo, however, had also ordered the embassy to destroy two of its three decoding machines, and embassy staff members were not particularly skilled at typing. As a result, the process of preparing the message for delivery took far longer than Japanese officials had intended.

As each part of the message was transmitted, it was intercepted by U.S. intelligence. Although much of official Washington was shut down on this peculiarly warm December Saturday, Colonel Rufus Bratton, head of Army Intelligence's Far East Section, and Lieutenant Commander Alwin D. Kramer in the Office of Naval Intelligence had been busy all day translating the obscure, rambling message as each section came through over the wires. By 8:00 that evening they had deciphered the first thirteen parts, but the final section had not yet been cabled by Tokyo. The sections they did have, however, were stern in tone, declaring that Japan could no longer "tolerate" British and American interference in Asia.

Secret Voyage to Hawaii

Japan's Strike Force Crosses the Pacific

After weeks of training exercises for the Pearl Harbor attack, the ships in Japan's Hawaii strike force returned to port in mid-November 1941, where they were loaded with fuel, ammunition, and supplies. Then, divided into inconspicuous groupings of two or three, they stealthily sailed north to a secret rendezvous point at cold, isolated Hitokappu Bay in the Kurile Islands.

There, under the command of Vice Admiral Chuichi Nagumo, the crews were told of their mission and received their instructions for the attack. For three days in that remote outpost, they trained for their assignments and made final preparations for their voyage. Crew members wrote letters to their families, and some donned the "thousand-stitch" belts they had been given for good fortune in battle. Made of white cloth, each belt, or *senninbari,* was embroidered with a thousand red knots hand-stitched by a thousand well-wishers.

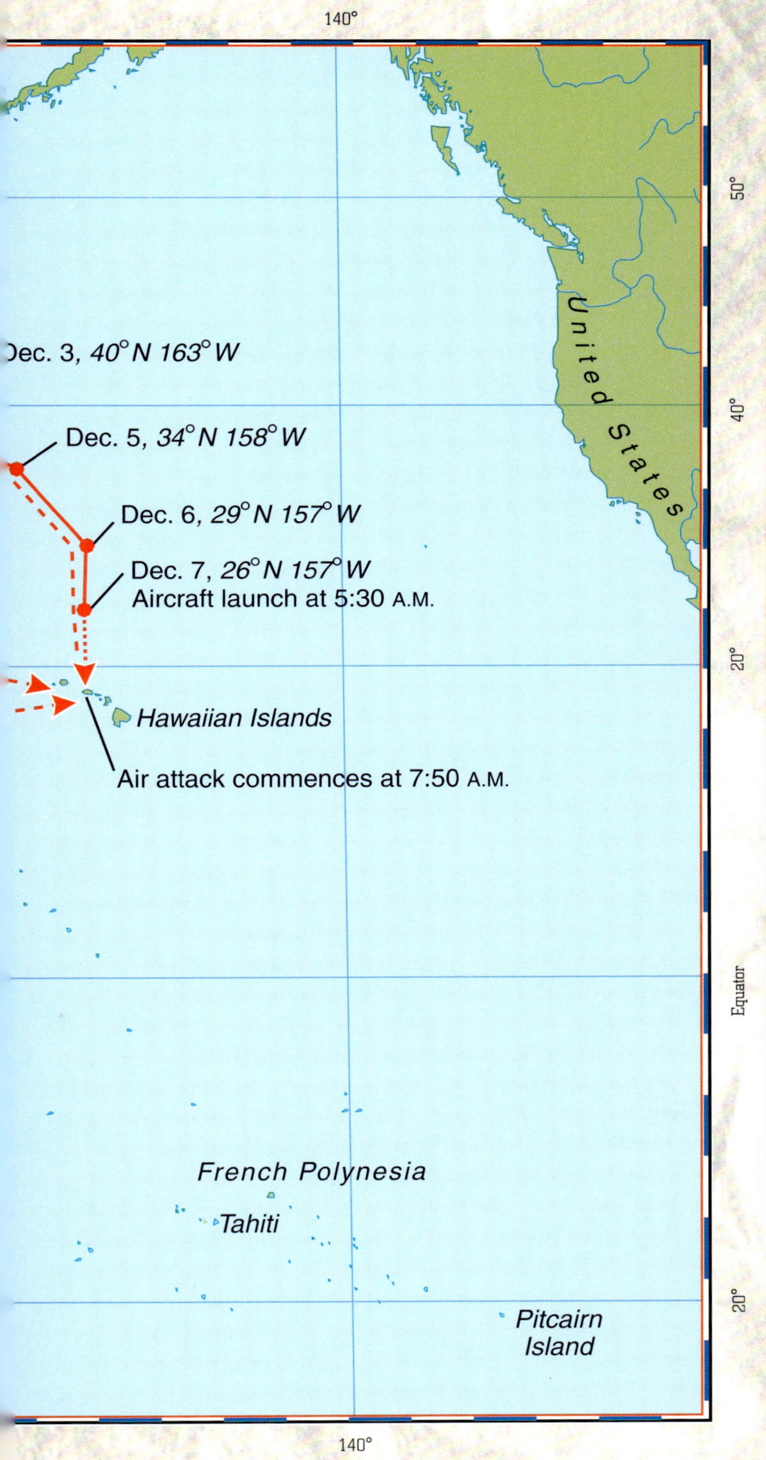

Attack route

While the carrier strike force headed southeast from the Kuriles to Hawaii, Japanese submarine squadrons secretly crossed the ocean to perform advance reconnaissance, launch midget submarine attacks, and destroy any enemy vessels that escaped and counterattacked the Japanese.

Nagumo's flagship

On the carrier *Akagi, below,* the ship's vital center of operations is protectively wrapped in splinter padding made of rolled-up mattresses. The range finder (*lower right*) is covered with coiled rope to prevent damage.

On Tuesday, November 25 (Hawaii time), the strike force sailed from Hitokappu Bay, beginning a more than four-thousand-mile northern crossing of the Pacific. Although few ships navigated in the ocean so far north—a fact that greatly improved the attack's chances of surprise—it was a risky route, since stormy winter weather could make refueling at sea nearly impossible. Weather conditions were, however, surprisingly good, despite rough seas, storms, and fog, and ocean refueling was accomplished smoothly. Throughout the voyage, strict radio silence was maintained; even the keys and fuses of the transmitters were removed.

On December 6, the warships arrived at a designated point some 650 miles north of Pearl Harbor. There, the crews were ordered to raise their speed and make their dash due south 420 miles to the launch point for the attack. Crew members received encouraging messages from Admiral Isoroku Yamamoto and the emperor, while on board Vice Admiral Nagumo's flagship *Akagi,* signal flags were raised, exhorting the fleet that the "fate of the Japanese Empire will depend upon the issue of this battle."

Arriving the next morning before dawn at the launch point, 230 miles north of Pearl Harbor, the crews manned their combat stations and made the last preparations for the attack, waving their caps to the planes as they launched one by one from the decks of the carriers and disappeared in waves into the southern sky.

Kramer was alarmed by the message and decided to get it to the president and navy chiefs without waiting for the missing fourteenth part. Bratton, who was responsible for reporting intelligence to top army brass, was less convinced that the multipart message was urgent enough to warrant delivery on a Saturday night.

Although Kramer sent six locked cases containing the messages to Bratton, the army specialist never got the documents into the hands of those who were supposed to receive them: General Marshall, Secretary of State Hull, and Secretary of War Stimson.

Kramer, however, made intensive efforts to deliver the dispatches immediately. At 9:00 P.M., Kramer's wife drove him from his Navy Department office to the White House, where he handed the sealed pouch to Lieutenant Lester Schulz and asked that he bring it to the president's attention immediately. Roosevelt received the pouch in the Oval Office, where he was meeting with his longtime personal adviser, Harry Hopkins. The president spent ten minutes reading over the message, while Hopkins paced the room. "This means war," Roosevelt said, after handing it to his old friend to read. The two men then discussed the situation in French Indochina, where they assumed Japan would strike.

After delivering the thirteen-part message to the president, Kramer continued on to Secretary Knox's apartment at the Wardman Park Hotel. After reading the Japanese communication, Knox phoned Secretary Stimson to schedule a meeting for the next morning. Kramer and his wife then drove across the river to Virginia to deliver the message to Naval Intelligence Chief Rear Admiral Theodore Stark Wilkinson, who was having dinner with his army counterpart, Brigadier General Sherman Miles. Miles, perusing the message, judged that it had "little military significance." Later that evening, he advised Bratton that the document was not urgent enough to justify waking General Marshall. Kramer completed his deliveries at the Maryland home of Rear Admiral Richard Kelly Turner, the

Battle of the Bands

Every two weeks since September 13, navy bands from the *Pennsylvania, California, Detroit, Tennessee, Arizona,* and *Argonne* faced off in the "Battle of Music" at the Bloch Arena, playing swing, ballad, and jitterbug numbers. On Saturday night, December 6, 1941, the battleship *Pennsylvania* won. The next morning, all of the members of the *Arizona*'s band perished in the attack. The "Battle of Music" trophy was given posthumously to the lost musicians of the battleship *Arizona*.

The "Battle of Music" Trophy

Navy's Chief of War Plans, around midnight. After reading the dispatch, Turner declined to take any action, stating that it was not his function to do so.

That night—Saturday, December 6—Honolulu was blazing with Christmas lights, its streets packed shoulder-to-shoulder with sailors, soldiers, and football fans who had crowded Honolulu Stadium for the annual Shrine game. At Pearl Harbor's Bloch Arena Recreation Center, Fleet musicians competed in the fierce "Battle of Music," with battleship *Pennsylvania* players taking the first prize. All over Honolulu and the military bases, parties and dances went on late into the night. Strolling through town on their way to a dance in Honolulu, Katherine Rodrigues and her husband, Dennis, walked past the Japanese consulate and saw smoke curiously coming from the complex. "We peeked through the fence and saw this guy burning papers in the back of the embassy," Katherine recalled—a strange thing, she thought, for someone to be doing so late at night.

Kimmel was out that evening, too, at a small dinner party with friends at the Halekulani Hotel. The admiral had been invited to the Japanese consulate for champagne, but he had declined the offer. Short and his wife were at a charity dinner dance at the Schofield Officers Club. They left the club before 11:00 P.M.; the lieutenant general had a 10:00 A.M. golf date with Kimmel the next morning. Approaching Pearl Harbor, they gazed out at the spectacular sight of the huge ships, their lights blinking in the dark like a colossal Christmas ornament. "What a target that would make," Short mused as they drove by.

At the same moment, over the Pacific, a dozen American B-17 Flying Fortress bombers were making the long flight from California to Hawaii, their first stop before they reached their final destination of Manila. For safety's sake on the twenty-four-hundred-mile journey, the planes carried a heavy load of fuel but no ammunition; their guns were carefully wrapped up and packed away. As the planes droned toward Honolulu, local radio station KGMB stayed on the air all night to give them a guiding signal. Ahead of them lay the great Pacific Fleet base of Pearl Harbor, its warships at rest, watertight compartments open and ready for inspection. That night, no offshore patrols surveyed the waters. Anti-aircraft guns had been disabled, their ammunition safely locked away. Fighter and patrol planes were parked quietly in rows at Hickam, Wheeler, Bellows, Kaneohe Bay, and Haleiwa, many with their guns removed and their gas tanks empty.

In the warm December night, navy bandsman Warren G. Harding relaxed after the hard-fought "Battle of the Bands." Standing on the fantail of the *California*, he watched a shower of meteors flash across the night sky over Pearl Harbor. As a boy, his grandfather had told him, "Every time you see a meteor fall, someone close to you is

B-17 bombers

Four-engine B-17 long-range bombers, known as "Flying Fortresses," were among the largest airplanes of their time. With a wingspan of more than one hundred feet, each B-17 was armed with machine guns and loaded with up to sixty-four hundred pounds of bombs. In the spring of 1941, the United States sent twenty of the heavy bombers to Britain under the Lend-Lease agreement. Secretary of War Henry Stimson believed that they were vital to the defense of the Philippines. On December 6, 1941, twelve B-17s left Hamilton Field near San Francisco for Hickam Field on Oahu, where they would stop to refuel on their way to Clark Field near Manila. They were expected to reach Pearl Harbor at 8:00 A.M. on Sunday, December 7.

going to die." Watching the meteors shooting through the dark, he couldn't help wondering to himself, "How many people do I know who are going to die soon?"

Silently, hundreds of miles north in the Pacific, the Japanese attack force sped steadily south toward Pearl Harbor. Now, on Vice Admiral Nagumo's carrier flagship *Akagi,* the "Z" signal flag flew from the mast. It was the same pennant that, thirty years earlier, had flown over Admiral Tojo's flagship before the battle of Tsushima, resulting in Japan's triumph over the Russians. The voyage east across the Pacific had been, in Yamamoto's words, "blessed by the War god"; refueling, his chief worry, had been accomplished easily. On December 2, the admiral had transmitted the fateful code, "Climb Mt. Niitaka," ordering his warships to proceed with the attack. The date of the Pearl Harbor strike—Sunday, December 7, Hawaii time—had been selected carefully. The moonlight would be favorable, Yamamoto judged; moreover, he knew that the fleet returned to harbor on weekends after training periods at sea, so there was great likelihood that most of the ships would be in port on Sunday morning. Now, on Saturday, December 6, Japan's intelligence confirmed that all of the battleships were indeed assembled at the Hawaiian base—although it was "most regrettable," operations officer Commander Minoru Genda noted, that none of the carriers would be in the harbor for the attack.

That night, as the sea swelled and rolled, four hundred planes—marked with the symbol of the

Toasting the mission

Carrier crew members toast the success of the surprise raid on Pearl Harbor. The day before the attack, observed Lieutenant Commander Sadao Chigusa, "was the last day which we could call peacetime." Crew members aboard his destroyer, the *Akigumo,* were treated to special food that day: raw apples and *Ohagi,* a dish made of sugar and red beans.

rising sun, parked wing-to-wing on the carrier decks—were carefully checked and loaded with torpedoes and bombs. Hundreds of miles south of the warships, the Japanese submarines were quietly surfacing outside Pearl Harbor in the Pacific. Five of them carried a special cargo: a two-man, battery-powered midget submarine. Released from their "mother" subs, the five miniature vessels would stealthily penetrate Pearl Harbor, launching their own deadly torpedo attacks once the air strike was underway. Although the plan called for the midget subs to escape after the attack and rendezvous with their mother ships, the two-man crews assumed they had no chance of survival. The teams were determined to achieve their mission, if necessary, by ramming themselves, and their torpedoes, against their targets.

As the mother ships assumed their launch positions, the crews of the small subs made their own last preparations. Ensign Kazuo Sakamaki wrote a farewell letter to his parents, attached the exact postage, and carefully wrapped it together with clippings of his hair and nails. He bathed, dressed, and said his good-byes aboard the mother ship. Although he knew that his vessel's gyroscope was broken, making his sub nearly impossible to navigate, Ensign Sakamaki was undeterred. Taking with them a pistol, a samurai sword, some food, and a bottle of wine, he and his crew mate, Chief Warrant Officer Kiyoshi Inagaki, climbed into their tiny craft and began their ten-and-a-half-mile underwater journey to Pearl Harbor.

AI301

Commander takes off

As crew members cheer in the predawn darkness on December 7, 1941, Commander Mitsuo Fuchida's plane roars down the deck of the carrier *Akagi* to lead the attack on Pearl Harbor. Fuchida's aircraft, a Nakajima B5N2 horizontal bomber, was later code-named a "Kate" bomber by the Allies. One hundred and three Kates loaded with bombs, as well as forty Kates armed with torpedoes, took off from the carriers that morning, heading for Pearl Harbor in two waves.

Painting by Tom Freeman.

Ready for battle

Flier Yoshio Shimezu, *right* (wearing a naval aviator uniform), took off from the aircraft carrier *Hiryu* the morning of the attack on board an Aichi dive bomber, code-named "Val" by the Allies.

In the ocean to the north, the six Japanese aircraft carriers pitched and rolled in high winds and rough seas in the deep blackness before dawn. Water washed over the decks, and crews clung to their planes to keep them from hurtling overboard. After receiving their orders to launch, the flying crews climbed into the planes and revved up the engines. The *Akagi* turned and headed into the north wind, raising its battle flag, and a swinging green lamp on the flight deck gave the signal for the first plane to take off. Roaring, the first fighter began its run down the carrier deck, nosing skyward just as the ship plunged suddenly into the surging seas. Within minutes, 183 fighters, bombers, and torpedo planes, the first wave of the Japanese strike force, were in the air. Circling proudly once over the great fleet, they turned and headed south to Pearl Harbor, guided only by the lights of the lead planes. It was Sunday morning. The time was 6:15 A.M.

Maintaining Strike-Force Morale

From the War Diary of Sadao Chigusa, Lieutenant Commander of the *Akigumo*

On November 16, 1941, the Japanese destroyer *Akigumo* left Kure Naval Base, beginning its long, secret voyage to Pearl Harbor as part of the *Kido Butai,* the imperial strike force. As executive officer and chief ordnance officer on the destroyer, Rear Admiral Sadao Chigusa faced the challenge of keeping his crew in peak condition during their long and often stormy ocean journey. In this diary excerpt, he explains how he kept his men primed for the attack.

As Executive Officer of the Akigumo *and in a sense "mother" of the ship, I had always wished that all our crew, that is, my children, could engage in this battle in good health. In plain language, that is, I took care of them in various ways, so they would not suffer from illness and not be wounded or swept away by the waves. As the* Akigumo *was a destroyer, we were especially fortunate to have a Naval surgeon on board. (A doctor usually was not on board each destroyer.)*

So I could feel a bit easy relying on the doctor if I had a patient on my ship. . . .

The methods used to maintain morale for which I worked hard were as follows:

The Strict Enforcement of Singing War Songs

We strictly enforced singing of war songs every day by all the crew gathered together on the open deck, so far as circumstances could permit. As for the songs, our Navy made it a habit to simply sing four or five commonplace songs at one time, but I made every effort to let them sing popular songs which I especially selected for the young sailors, who raised their voices from the bottom of their hearts for over a half hour. . . . We couldn't achieve the purpose of our singing until all the crew would positively attend it with great pleasure. . . .

By Seizing an Opportunity to Give Enough Time (Nearly One-Third of a Day) for Their Recreation

It was a regulation to permit the crew amusement and music only on Sunday and on festivals when we are aboard ship in normal times. But it was necessary to consider their need for recreation, permitting it, if possible, every day even in wartime when we are on such a long, weary voyage. And we usually beamed the radio news and entertainment from Japan throughout the ship on such occasions.

The Strict Enforcement of Gymnastics

It was very difficult to force gymnastics on the crew at the same time, utilizing the narrow deck of a destroyer, particularly when operating in stormy weather. But I did my best to give them such diversions under all possible conditions. I also added games they liked as much as I could, so as to give the sailors a happy familiarity with gymnastics. (Some sailors reacted passively to gymnastics when we had only formal exercise.)

Methods for Buttressing Morale by Food

Giving enjoyment to sailors infuses life into them and cuts mental fatigue. On the sea, the life of every serious day can't be enjoyable without good meals. It was very important to have a good menu for the sailors, so as to give enjoyment to their meals.

Although it was no easy task to plan good menus in such bad situations as limited food budgets and limited storage capacity for food, I did my best to urge our cooks to do so. The many sweet and special foods prepared for our midnight supper of which I wrote in my diary were no exception to this consideration. When I served Ohagi *with two apples to all the crew for their lunch on the day before "X" Day [the day of the attack], I could distinctly see the sailors' determination to do their best with real pleasure.*

When we lived on the sea during a long voyage, watching for our enemy, we used to become demoralized without knowing it. Stormy weather also gives a stimulus to it. How to help the sailors keep their original pep is a problem before meeting any enemy, and we seriously considered it. If a sailor is dead tired before meeting his enemy, he cannot fully utilize his fighting strength. . . .

Seafaring living is unnatural [for human beings], and . . . the longer we continue our seafaring lives, the more we interfere with our health. We must consider how we can keep our potential, that is, our physical strength. At least we must keep strong by all means until we meet our enemy.

Reprinted with permission from *The Pearl Harbor Papers*, edited by Donald M. Goldstein and Katherine V. Dillon (New York: Brassey's, 1993).

The carrier strike force

The *Soryu* was one of six aircraft carriers in the *Kido Butai*, Japan's Pearl Harbor strike force. This aft view shows the underside of the flight deck and the wake created by the massive ship. The other carriers in the secret Pacific convoy that sailed across the Pacific to Hawaii were the *Kaga, Hiryu, Shokaku, Zuikaku,* and the flagship, the *Akagi*. The Japanese carrier force was screened by nine destroyers and one light cruiser, supported by two battleships and two heavy cruisers, supplied by eight oilers, and escorted by a patrol force of three submarines.

Twilight at Pearl Harbor

The sun sets over the Pacific Fleet's battleships, moored together in the shelter of Pearl Harbor.

WARD

ATTACK!

In the hours before dawn on Sunday, December 7, the great gray warships rested, still and quiet, in the waters of Pearl Harbor. The last crew members had made it back to their vessels from shore leave and were settled in their berths asleep. Just outside the silent base, Japanese submarines prowled, unseen, in the Pacific, some lurking less than nine miles outside the harbor's mouth. Most of the five midget submarines had left their mother ships and were slowly, stealthily making their way into the port.

At 3:54 A.M., Ensign R. C. McCloy, on patrol off Pearl Harbor on board the U.S. minesweeper Condor, *noticed what he thought was the periscope of a submarine some two miles from the harbor's entrance. The sub came within fifty yards of the minecraft, then abruptly turned and headed in the opposite direction. By blinker light, the* Condor *communicated the suspicious sighting to the* Ward, *a reconditioned World War I–era destroyer that was also patrolling the sea approaches to Pearl Harbor. The* Ward *scoured the area for signs of the submarine, without success.*

At 4:46 A.M., the harbor's large antisubmarine gate swung wide open to let the minesweeper *Crossbill* enter the base. Since the *Condor* was expected to pass through at around 5:30, and the tug *Keosanqua* some forty-five minutes later, the gate stayed open, even though it was supposed to be closed throughout the night.

At 6:30 A.M., as the first shadows of morning crossed the water, the *Ward* spotted a small, green, cigar-shaped sub that appeared to be following the supply ship *Antares,* its barnacle-and-moss-covered conning tower jutting just two feet above the water. A Navy PBY seaplane—one of three patroling the east, south, and west sectors of Oahu—dropped float lights over the submarine to mark its position, and at 6:45, the *Ward*'s skipper, Lieutenant William W. Outerbridge, ordered his crew to open fire. From his view on the *Antares,* Fireman Third Class William Ellis saw "the destroyer . . . blasting the conning tower off the sub" with a four-inch gun, firing two shots and dropping depth charges. Lieutenant Outerbridge reported the action to the Fourteenth Naval District watch officer: "We have attacked, fired upon, and dropped depth charges upon submarine operating in defensive area." About half an hour later, the message was finally decoded, and a duty officer informed Rear Admiral Claude C. Bloch of the contact. Bloch was not overly concerned by the report; there had already been false sightings of submarines in the area, and whales had occasionally been depth-charged by mistake. He ordered the destroyer *Monaghan* to go out and verify the

The first shot

At 6:45 A.M. on Sunday, December 7, the destroyer *Ward* opens fire on a two-man Japanese submarine spotted just outside the entrance to Pearl Harbor. The four-inch shell, the first shot fired in the Pacific War, just misses the conning tower of the midget sub, one of five launched by the Japanese that morning as part of their surprise attack. At 6:53 A.M., the *Ward* succeeded in sinking the intruder.

Painting by Tom Freeman.

Pillow cover from the USS Arizona

situation. At around 7:30 A.M., Admiral Husband E. Kimmel also learned of the sighting. He said that he would be "right down" but was not alarmed; he planned to wait for verification of the report.

Meanwhile, as the sun began to rise over the Pacific, the strike force of 183 Japanese attack planes soared south over the ocean toward their target. Commander Mitsuo Fuchida flew at the lead of forty-nine high-level bombers, each carrying a deadly 1,786-pound, armor-piercing bomb. Cruising beneath him were forty torpedo planes, loaded with specially adapted, shallow-water torpedoes. Above him soared fifty-one dive bombers and forty-three swift fighter planes, flying cover for the attackers as they droned over thick clouds, more than 9,000 feet above the ocean. As the morning brightened, Fuchida opened his cockpit canopy and gazed back at the planes behind him, their wings flashing silver in the brilliant sunlight. Then, tuning his radio to station KGMB in Honolulu—the same station that was guiding the American B-17 bombers from the coast—he homed in on the signal and listened, relieved, to the weather report from Honolulu: visibility good; wind north, ten knots. "A more favorable situation could not have been imagined," he recalled.

Photo found in wreckage

Zeros take off

Fighters and high-level bombers warm up in preparation for takeoff on the deck of the Japanese aircraft carrier *Shokaku*. Japan's Mitsubishi A6M2 fighters, known to the Allies as "Zeros," were known for their lightness, range, and maneuverability. Armed with two 7.7-millimeter and two twenty-millimeter machine guns, they could reach a speed of 340 miles per hour and were the fastest fighters in the sky. Zeros had already demonstrated their deadly air power in the China war. After taking off from the carriers for Pearl Harbor, they would fly at 14,100 feet above the bombers, protecting them against attacks from enemy planes.

Far below, at Kahuku Point on the northern tip of Oahu, two army privates, Joseph Lockard and George Elliott, were idly passing time as they manned their experimental mobile radar set, the only unit working on the island that morning. Their Opana radar station usually only operated between 4:00 A.M. and 7:00 A.M. on weekends, but the two decided to keep the set going this Sunday morning while they waited for their breakfast to arrive. Just after 7:00, the screen lit up with blips showing a huge flight of approaching planes, approximately 132 miles to the north. Lockard quickly relayed the information by phone to First Lieutenant Kermit A. Tyler, a pursuit officer trainee on duty at the Fort Shafter Information Center. "Don't worry about it," Tyler told him, certain that the privates had picked up the flight of B-17s coming in as expected from California.

Overhead, the Japanese planes were now quickly closing in on the island. As Fuchida searched for signs of Oahu's coast, the thick cloud cover suddenly broke, and a long, white line of coast appeared. At 7:40 A.M., Fuchida fired one shot from his signal pistol, and the planes surrounding him maneuvered into formation—dive bombers soaring to fifteen thousand feet, torpedo bombers swooping low over the island, and horizontal bombers skimming just under the clouds. At 7:49, Fuchida signaled by radio, *"To! To! To! . . . ,"* the order to begin the strike; within minutes, the attack force began pounding the airfields to shatter the island's aerial defenses. Japanese fighters and bombers screamed over Kaneohe Bay Naval Air Station, blasting thirty new PBY scout planes. Twenty-five dive bombers devastated Wheeler Field, the largest army fighter plane base in the Pacific. With arms and ammunition locked away, soldiers were unable to fire back as the attackers relentlessly struck Wheeler's 140 fighters. At nearby Schofield Barracks, Sergeant Emil Matula grabbed a fire ax and chopped his way through locked supply rooms and gun racks to grab weapons. But by the time he had a few machine guns ready to fire, the attack was nearly over—the main hangars at Wheeler had been leveled, and all the planes had been destroyed where they sat parked outside their protective bunkers in the field.

Burning planes
Navy PBY patrol seaplanes go up in flames at Kaneohe Bay Naval Air Station after hits by Japanese fighters and bombers.

Meanwhile, two squadrons of Japanese fighters were streaking back and forth at two hundred miles an hour across Ewa Marine Corps Air Station, obliterating its forty-eight aircraft; other raiders swarmed over the rows of B-17s and B-18s sitting out in the open at Hickam Field. Swooping low, they strafed Hickam's quadrangles and dropped a bomb through a mess hall roof, wiping out thirty-five men. One marine, First Lieutenant Cornelius C. Smith Jr., watched from his barracks near Hickam as men stumbled out, wide-eyed, dazed, some dressed, some lurching into pants and shirts on the run, a few in towels, screaming at each other to take cover. All the time, he remembered, bombs were whistling to earth, detonating with ear-shattering explosions, flashing silver in the sun like falling snowflakes.

Overhead, as columns of smoke rose from Wheeler Field and Kaneohe Bay, Fuchida gazed out from his plane over the peaceful, still slumbering harbor. Not a single U.S. Army or Navy plane was in the air. Assured of the success of his attack, Fuchida had signaled the code confirming that the attack was a surprise, *"Tora! Tora! Tora! . . . ."* Now, he banked his plane sharply as ten squadrons formed a "gorgeous formation" behind him, he recalled, a single, deadly column of planes, two hundred meters apart, ready to strike savagely at the Pacific Fleet.

Below them, on Battleship Row, the great ships were quietly lined up in their berths along Ford Island. Six of the vessels were moored in pairs—the *Oklahoma* was tied up with the *Maryland,* the *Arizona* with the repair ship *Vestal,* and the *Tennessee* with the *West Virginia.* The *California* and the *Nevada* were moored alone. Only one of the ninety-four warships, the destroyer *Helm,* was on the move in the harbor that morning. Aboard the others, sailors were just beginning to stir, sipping coffee, showering, shaving, eating breakfast, lounging on the decks, playing checkers, writing Christmas cards. The sound of church bells drifted over the harbor on the breeze. On the *Nevada,* at 7:55 A.M., the ship's band assembled in position on the deck, ready to strike up "The Star-Spangled Banner," while a marine color guard prepared to raise the flag. At that moment, Commander Logan Ramsey in the Ford Island Naval Air Station

Bombed air field
Smoke billows from Wheeler Field, where Japanese planes attacked hangars, destroyed army fighter aircraft, strafed residences, and blasted the airbase's PX and firehouse. "The next day," recalled Staff Sergeant Stephen Koran, "a fellow could sit out on the flight line and cry" to see bulldozers push what was left of the planes into three piles nearly forty feet high.

Attack on Ewa Air Field

A Japanese fighter from the carrier *Kaga,* sweeps low over Ewa Marine Corp Air Station, exploding aircraft and shattering fire trucks and automobiles as marines run to salvage damaged planes and equipment. *Painting by Tom Freeman.*

operations center saw a plane swoop low outside his window, then heard an explosion as Japanese attackers bombed the base's twenty-nine patrol planes and blasted the hangars, which were "burning like a forest fire," he recalled. Ramsey raced to the radio room and barked out a warning: "AIR RAID PEARL HARBOR. THIS IS NO DRILL." Then, as the twenty-three bandsmen on the *Nevada* launched into the first notes of the national anthem, two Japanese planes skimmed over the battleship, splintering the deck and shredding the flag just as it ran up the pole. The musicians stayed in position, playing the anthem to the end, then scrambled for cover as men all over the ship raced to their battle stations at the guns, in the bridge, at damage control posts, and in the engine rooms.

On the battleship *West Virginia,* nicknamed the *WeeVee,* six aerial torpedoes struck suddenly, collapsing decks, knocking out lights and communications, and sending plumes of suffocating yellow smoke throughout the ship. Water rushed in through gaping holes on her port side, as panicked men pleaded and screamed and the vessel listed twenty-eight degrees. Lieutenant Claude V. Ricketts started counterflooding measures, at last righting her with a fifteen-degree list as she sank onto the muddy harbor bottom.

On the *Tennessee,* moored beside the *West Virginia,* seventeen-year-old Jack Evans watched a Japanese plane dive in so low that he could see the frightened crew member in the rear gripping the seat in front of him. On the *Oklahoma,* just ahead, Adolph Mortenson was sleeping soundly after late-night duty when he head a voice over the loudspeaker hollering, "This is a real air raid, no shit!" Wearing only his pajama bottoms, he raced for his battle station in the boiler room as the ship jumped under his feet from torpedoes striking deep inside the hull. Lights went out, and a phonograph somewhere was playing the song "Let Me Off Uptown" as lockers, dishes, tables, and eight-foot reels of cable careened wildly about the ship. Fourteen-hundred-pound shells rolled free as the ship listed, crushing men caught helpless in their path. Water surged through the *Oklahoma*'s wounds, through wide-open watertight compartments, through open hatches and ventilator shafts, and through its open blisters. As it rushed into the compartments below decks, sailors grabbed clothes, blankets, anything they could find to try to stop the flooding. It was no use.

Devastation on Ford Island

Japanese fighters and bombers destroyed planes and hangars at the Ford Island Naval Air Station. At 7:57 A.M., an alert was radioed from the station: "AIR RAID PEARL HARBOR. THIS IS NO DRILL." From the shelter of a ditch on Ford Island, Chief Petty Officer Thomas Forrow watched "the explosions of torpedoes, the bombs bursting, the fires, the dense black smoke from the oil, ships going over."

As the battleship filled quickly with seawater, men gasped for air and tried to swim free of the ship, which was now starting to roll over, burying its masts into the harbor mud. Within minutes, the *Oklahoma* had settled bottom up at a thirty-degree angle. Sailors who were topside crawled onto her keel in a hail of bullets and bombs, while down below, inside the *Oklahoma*'s hull, trapped sailors struggled to save themselves in a wild, dark chaos of rising water and tumbling objects—"like turning a motel upside down," seaman William Fomby remembered.

Battleship Row

Clouds of black smoke hang over bombed Battleship Row, where the *Maryland (far left)* is flooding, the *Oklahoma* has capsized, and the *West Virginia* is sinking and burning beside the *Tennessee*.

Adolph Mortenson found himself in the medical dispensary—its tile floor now the ceiling—with four other men and only a small pocket of air above the water. With his feet, he found an eleven-inch porthole beneath the surface and dived down to open it, helping three men to escape. As the air supply in the compartment dwindled rapidly, Mortenson recalled, "the ship's carpenter . . . a large man weighing over two hundred pounds, knew he'd never make it through the porthole." With only a few minutes of oxygen left, the carpenter reached down and held the porthole open for Mortenson, who was barely able to squeeze his body through the opening. Other men, elsewhere on the ship, including seaman Stephen Bower Young, remained trapped inside the hull for hours longer, listening to the groans of twisting metal and the moans and

Aerial attack

This photograph of Pearl Harbor, taken from a Japanese plane, shows a torpedo striking the battleship *Oklahoma (center).* Nine torpedoes hit the vessel, flooding the *Oklahoma* and causing her to capsize in the harbor.

labored breathing of fellow sailors struggling for life. Beating hammers, wrenches, and hands against the bulkheads, they banged out SOS signals in the dark until some were rescued and others lost their lives.

On the battleship *California,* an awning was being set up for church services when crewman Glen Turner heard the roaring of a plane overhead and thought nothing of it. Then, suddenly, he heard explosions on Ford Island and the loudspeaker screaming, "Man your battle stations—this is no drill!" As Turner raced to his post near a .50-caliber anti-aircraft machine gun, the *California* was coming under attack. The gunner's mates pounded on the locked ammunition box to open it, only to find that it was empty. Crewmen passed ammunition hand-over-hand from the ammunition lockers to the guns, Turner recalled, but it was well into the attack before any of them were able to start shooting.

Ripped open by two aerial torpedoes, the *California* was flooding quickly through its wide-open hatches and manhole covers. Bandsman Warren G. Harding had hurried to his battle post in a forward repair area below decks, as the ship leapt from torpedo hits as though it had been "picked up in the water." Staying at his station to maintain watertight integrity, even after the order was given to abandon ship, Harding lay at his post in the water with six other men—electricians, shipfitters, and another musician—waiting and hoping for rescue. Somebody had a pencil, and as the time ticked by, Harding remembered, each man scrawled his will out on the bulkheads.

Sinking the USS *California*

With her watertight compartments wide open for inspection, the battleship *California* flooded rapidly and started listing after taking three torpedo hits. When a torpedo strikes, "it feels like the battleship is picked up in the water, then it kind of shakes and settles back down," recalled one crew member on the *California*. "You could have driven a Mack truck through either one of the torpedo holes."

At the other end of Battleship Row, on the *Arizona,* seaman Martin Matthews had put on his dress whites, since he planned to do some sightseeing around the island. Only fifteen years old—he had lied to the navy about his age—Matthews heard some planes coming in, but nobody, he remembered, paid any attention. "At first, we didn't realize it was a bombing," recalled Seaman Second Class George Phraner. Then he and others saw the rising sun emblem on the planes. As the attackers dived over the ship—some so close that sailors could have hit them with hand grenades—Phraner raced to his battle station at the forward five-inch gun. Bombs struck the ship astern, and as Private First Class James Cory recalled, "You could feel the decks . . . being penetrated" like a needle piercing taut pieces of cloth. It was a bomb exploding in the bow of the ship, however, that sealed the *Arizona*'s fate. At 8:06 A.M., an armor-piercing payload dropped 10,440 feet, right down through the ship's forecastle, instantly igniting more than a million pounds of explosives stored in the forward magazines. Cory remembered hearing "a very heavy slap" when the bomb hit. Phraner, far down in the ship looking for ammunition, heard "a deafening roar . . .

Clock recovered from USS Arizona

Run for the sea

At 8:45 A.M., the damaged *Nevada* began a valiant effort to escape the harbor, but came under heavy attack by dive bombers and fighters during the second wave. Although the Japanese tried to sink the *Nevada*, blocking the entrance to the harbor, the ship's crew managed to beach her out of harm's way. *Painting by Tom Freeman.*

the entire ship shuddered." In seconds, a colossal fireball burst five hundred feet into the air with a blast so powerful that it blew men off the decks of the *Nevada,* the *Vestal,* and the *West Virginia.* Ammunition, shells, lockers, timber, bits of steel, and fragments of human flesh and bone rained over the ship. Hundreds died instantly in the flash of flame, including every member of the *Arizona*'s band and the ship's commanding officer, Captain Franklin Van Valkenburgh. The only trace remaining of Admiral Isaac C. Kidd, Battleship Division One Commander, was his gold class ring, fused to the steel conning tower on the ship.

The *Arizona* lurched in the air, then buckled and collapsed. The lights went out, and thick, acrid smoke filled the magazine locker below decks where Phraner had been hunting for ammunition. As he made his way up through the ship, he was nauseated by the smell of his own flesh, which was burning from the searingly hot metal of the ladder. Surrounded by choking smoke and the moans and sounds of falling bodies, he felt increasingly weak and lightheaded as he clung to the ladder for support. Glimpsing a small point of light through the smoke, he climbed toward it. Gasping for air, he finally reached the upper deck and breathed deeply to clear his lungs and head. He saw nothing but a giant wall of flame and smoke as he looked toward the forward end of the ship. "There were dead men all around me," Phraner recalled. Behind him, a marine lay on the deck, his body split in two. Others were burning alive, stumbling silently out of the towering sheet of flames.

Cringing behind the massive structure of Turret No. III, James Cory had felt the heat and power of the blast. Now, in a nightmarish scene, he saw men wandering aimlessly like "zombies," he remembered, burned completely white as though covered with paint, their hair and eyebrows gone; the insoles of their shoes were their only remaining charred scraps of clothing. Stumping along the flaming decks, "they were moving like robots," Cory remembered, "their arms . . . out, held away from their bodies." Seeing men on fire, gasping for air, boatswain's mate Joseph George, aboard the *Vestal,* threw a line over to some sailors who were desperately trying to escape the blazing *Arizona.* One badly burned seaman, Donald Stratton, and five other sailors grabbed the line and managed to swing themselves hand-over-hand to the *Vestal,* while other sailors vanished in the flames. Seaman Clay Musick was able to escape by stepping off the listing *Arizona*'s two-foot-wide gangway onto the quay, just before it collapsed into the water. Cory dove off the burning *Arizona* into the harbor. As strafer fire splashed around him,

The USS Arizona

No ship suffered greater damage or loss of life than the *Arizona.* Moored next to the repair ship *Vestal* on Battleship Row, the *Arizona* was pounded by Japanese bombers in the first minutes of the attack. Two bombs scored direct hits. One exploded deep within the vessel, igniting its forward ammunition magazines. In the blinding flash and searing flames that consumed the ship, 1,177 men lost their lives. The explosion was so violent that it blew sailors off nearby ships into the water, and oil fires from the *Arizona* threatened other vessels in the harbor.

Life preserver from the No. 2 motor launch of the USS Arizona

Anti-aircraft fire

During the second-wave attack, intense American anti-aircraft fire battered Japanese planes, and thick smoke obscured their targets.

"you could feel the impact of the bullets," he remembered; "there was a tremendous amount of confusion and noise." The air was thick with smoke and bursting shells, and the *Arizona*'s oil began moving toward him, congealing and bursting into flames, turning the surface of the harbor into a sea of fire.

On the other side of Ford Island, the target ship *Utah* was badly crippled by two torpedo hits. As she listed rapidly, the heavy six-by-twelve-foot timbers covering her deck crashed loose, and by 8:12 A.M., the ship had turned bottom-up, trapping dozens of crew members inside. The *Raleigh,* moored just behind the *Utah,* was luckier. A torpedo had ripped open the side of the ship, but the crew's fast counterflooding kept her from turning over. The ship's luck held later when an armor-piercing bomb crashed right through her without exploding until it struck the harbor bottom. None of the *Raleigh*'s men died in the attack. At the Navy Yard, meanwhile, the light cruiser *Helena* and minelayer *Oglala* suffered heavy damage. A torpedo rammed into the *Helena,* causing massive flooding, and its blast ruptured the *Oglala*'s plates. A bomb then exploded between the two ships, causing further, fatal flooding in the *Oglala*.

Doomed ships

The *Arizona*'s forward magazines explode, *above.* In a painting by Tom Freeman, *far right,* sailors trapped for twenty-five hours in the overturned *Oklahoma* finally see daylight as rescuers cut a hole in the ship's plates.

Log from the USS Arizona

Across the water, Ensign Ted Hechler Jr., on board the light cruiser *Phoenix,* saw a sky now "filled with diving planes and the black bursts of exploding anti-aircraft shells." The harbor was a riot of explosions and gunfire, and the crew of the *St. Louis* was shooting fiercely at the attacking planes. They "knew what was up, knew what to do and did it," remembered Captain George A. Rood—just like in a drill, according to Commander A. L. Seton, except for the "outbursts of cheering every time a plane was hit."

By 8:30 A.M., the first wave of Japanese attackers, their mission completed, turned and soared back toward their carriers, leaving Pearl Harbor filled with the burning, smoking hulks of broken ships. In the brief lull after the attack, as men struggled, trapped, in the sea of burning oil, the *Nevada*—with a forty-foot torpedo gash in her side—somehow managed to get up enough steam to head for open waters. As she made for the sea, passing close to the blazing *Arizona,* a second attack wave of 171 Japanese fighters and bombers droned over the island, targeting the airfields and least-damaged ships inside the harbor. Swarms of dive bombers now pounded the *Nevada* fiercely as they tried to sink her in the narrow channel. The *Nevada*'s crew quickly realized the danger. As the battleship's gunners fired at the attackers, her acting commander deliberately grounded the ship to keep her from blocking the entrance to the harbor.

As the second wave of Japanese attackers reached their targets, the twelve B-17 bombers were flying into Oahu from California. Short of fuel and fired at by both sides during the chaos,

most of the pilots managed to land their planes at the burning airfields. Eighteen dive bombers from the carrier *Enterprise* also flew into the action. Twelve of the planes were able to land safely; five of them were shot out of the sky by the Japanese; and one dive bomber was gunned down by American fire. As the strike force launched its second, furious attack on the air bases—blasting planes, hangars, and repair facilities at Hickam, Kaneohe Bay, Ewa, and Bellows—a handful of American fliers were able to get their planes into the air. Second Lieutenants Kenneth Taylor and George Welch flew off in P-40 pursuit planes, fighting more than a dozen Japanese bombers over Oahu. Between them, they shot down six Japanese planes and damaged three. First Lieutenant Lewis Sanders led four planes into a flight of six Japanese fighters, knocking out one of the enemy planes, and Lieutenant Philip Rasmussen shot down an attacking airplane in a dogfight. On the ground, soldiers were now firing back at the Japanese planes with automatic rifles, pistols, and any other kinds of weapons they could find.

Surrounded by antiaircraft shooting and blinded by clouds of heavy smoke, the Japanese fliers now took aim at the

Megaphone from the USS Oklahoma

Freeing survivors

Rescue teams climb onto the capsized hull of the *Oklahoma,* working to free men trapped inside. One rescuer, Lieutenant Commander William M. Hobby, senior officer on board the *Oklahoma* when the attack began, remained on top of the hull for more than sixty hours. By tapping and banging on the ship's plates, survivors tried to signal their location to rescuers, who then cut holes in the hull in attempts to reach them. Rescue teams ultimately freed thirty-one men from the overturned battleship. The last survivor left the vessel two days after the attack, on the morning of December 9. A total of 415 men perished aboard the *Oklahoma.*

vessels in the navy dry docks. The destroyers *Cassin* and *Downes* exploded into flame, and the *Cassin* careened over onto the *Downes*. The *Pennsylvania* escaped serious damage, but the *Shaw,* helpless with her ammunition stowed away, took three bomb hits, the last one rupturing her oil tanks, igniting her forward ammunition magazines, and turning the vessel into a towering fireball.

As Japanese planes swarmed over the harbor, men crawled onto the upturned *Oklahoma* and *Utah,* trying desperately to free those trapped inside. One sailor from the *Maryland,* gunner George Waller recalled, climbed onto the bottom of the *Oklahoma* with a cutting torch and hoses, burning holes into the plates while planes were attacking all around him. On the *Utah,* a welder from the *Tangier* stayed at his task cutting holes while "planes were flying overhead and shrapnel from bombs and exploding shells and machine gun fire from the planes were falling," a crew mate recalled. After two tries, he managed to pull a twenty-year-old seaman from the upturned ship. Fifty-eight other men remained entombed inside.

At last, at around 10:00 A.M., the second attack wave finished its mission. As the fighters and bombers turned and left their targets, flying north toward the waiting carriers, Fuchida—the last to leave the scene—circled once more over Pearl Harbor to survey the smoldering effects of the attack. Below him, twenty-one vessels, including seven of the Pacific Fleet's great battleships, were sunk or badly damaged.

Saving survivors

Rescuers on a motor boat search the harbor by the overturned hull of the *Oklahoma*. Dodging bullets and oil fires, dozens of small boats set out during and after the attack to find survivors. Ken Haney, a crewman on the *Detroit,* went out on a boat along Battleship Row, picking up men who had been blown over the side of their ships. "The water caught fire," he recalled. "We stayed as long as we could, but . . . the coxswain said we had to get out of there or we wouldn't be able to save anybody. That was probably the worst moment for me," he said, leaving those men as the flames swept over the water.

In the airfields, 323 planes were shattered on the ground, crippled or totally destroyed. More than three thousand Americans were dead or wounded, while Fuchida's force had lost only nine fighters, five torpedo planes, and fifteen dive bombers—a toll that was far smaller than expected. At Pearl Harbor, Lieutenant Commander Sadao Chigusa reflected later, Japan's strike force had "made brilliant achievements."

Far below in the burning harbor, American rescuers set out in a tiny flotilla of launches and whaleboats, struggling to pull sailors, living and dead, out of the blazing water. Marine private Leslie Le Fan and Richard Fiske, a marine bugler from the *West Virginia,* were two of those who helped pull hundreds of burned and blasted bodies from the flames. The men were covered with black oil; some were missing limbs; many were burned beyond recognition. "It was an awe-inspiring sight," Le Fan recalled, "but it was devastating"—the closest, Fiske thought, that there could be to hell on earth.

Oil-soaked bill recovered from the California *during the salvage of ships*

Rescue boats

Aboard a motor launch, rescuers pull a survivor from the blazing water alongside the *West Virginia*. The torpedo-blasted battleship, her decks awash, has sunk into the muddy bottom of the harbor.

Dogfights over Oahu

At 7:51 A.M., Japanese fighters and dive bombers attacked Wheeler Field, home to 140 U.S. fighter planes. Two pilots, Second Lieutenants George Welch and Kenneth Taylor, saw the Japanese planes soaring by from the Wheeler Field officer's club, where they were attending an all-night party.

At first, Taylor thought they were navy planes—until they started shooting bullets into the club's walls and at the parked planes on the field. Still in their tuxedoes, the two fliers raced to Taylor's car, dodging strafer fire, and sped to Haleiwa Field, an air strip eleven miles away where they had parked their pursuit planes. Once airborne, the pilots attacked a swarm of Japanese dive bombers blasting the airbase below.

"We had absolutely no trouble at all finding plenty of targets," Taylor remembered. Welch's machine guns were disconnected, but he managed to fire his .30-caliber guns, claiming two Japanese planes. Taylor, wounded by enemy fire in the arm and leg, also shot down two planes before he and Welch flew back to Wheeler to refuel.

While the two pilots were on the ground, the second wave of Japanese raiders roared in, targeting their airplanes on the runway. Taylor and Welch managed to get airborne again and took off into the middle of the attacking swarm. Despite heavy gunfire damage to his plane, Welch shot down two more Japanese aircraft.

Other American fighter pilots, perhaps as many as twenty, took off after the raiders, too. Second Lieutenant Gordon Sterling was in the air, gunning at one Japanese plane with another enemy shooting at his tail. Although Sterling's plane burst into flames, the American continued firing, while another pilot, First Lieutenant Lewis Sanders, shot at his pursuer. All four planes fell into a vertical dive; Sanders was the only pilot who survived the fight.

Other "eagles of Wheeler," including First Lieutenant Robert Rogers and Second Lieutenant Philip Rasmussen, shot down Japanese planes over Oahu, while many defenders fired at the raiders from the ground. In the course of the Pearl Harbor assault, the Japanese lost fifteen dive bombers, nine fighters, and five torpedo planes.

Eagles of Wheeler

Second Lieutenants George Welch, *below,* and Kenneth Taylor took off in pursuit planes during the attack and shot down the first Japanese planes of the Pacific War. The two army air force pilots received the Distinguished Service Cross. American and Japanese fighters, *right,* clash in the skies above Oahu. *Painting by Tom Freeman.*

155
14
14

COURAGE IN THE LINE OF DUTY

On December 7, 1941, boys became men, and men became heroes, as President George Bush observed fifty years later. Thousands of those in Pearl Harbor that morning, and on nearby military bases, showed extraordinary courage in the face of sudden, unforeseen chaos and carnage. Sixteen of them were honored with Medals of Honor for their selfless actions, and many others have been commended and remembered for their bravery.

On the battleship *Oklahoma,* after torpedoes ripped the hull and seawater flooded the ship, twenty-two-year-old Ensign Francis Flaherty and twenty-year-old Seaman First Class James Ward stayed at their posts after the order had been given to abandon ship. Holding flashlights so that other members of their gun turret crew could see to escape, Flaherty and Ward willingly stayed behind, knowing that the vessel was going to capsize, and paid for their bravery with their lives.

Under attack, the target ship Utah, too, was flooding rapidly. Chief Watertender Peter Tomich, forty-eight, was at his battle station in the engineering plant when he realized that the ship was capsizing. Tomich stayed where he was, making sure that other crew members in the fireroom

Bravery under fire

In 1963, twenty-one years after the Pearl Harbor attack, Admiral Chester Nimitz *(third from left)* awards a Navy Commendation medal to Lieutenant Commander Glenn Decker *(far left)*. Decker was honored for his courage in maintaining a constant flow of communication from the exposed signal tower at Pearl Harbor during the Japanese attack.

Serving with honor

Mess Attendant First Class Doris Miller, *right,* received the Navy Cross, the navy's highest medal, for his courageous service at Pearl Harbor. In 1973, the destroyer escort *Miller* was commissioned in his honor, the third naval ship named for an African American.

evacuated and that all boilers were secured. Tomich perished with others on board the overturned vessel.

On the battleship *California,* bomb and torpedo hits crippled mechanized hoists that fed ammunition to the anti-aircraft guns. Radio Electrician Thomas Reeves, forty-six, voluntarily stayed inside a burning passageway, passing ammunition by hand to the ship's guns, until he was overcome and killed by smoke and fire.

Meanwhile, as the Japanese blasted ships on Battleship Row, a fragment of one bomb on the *Tennessee* struck the captain of the *West Virginia,* Mervyn S. Bennion. Mortally wounded in the stomach, Bennion stayed alert on the bridge, questioning others about the condition of the ship and efforts to combat the spreading fires. Finally, as flames and smoke engulfed the bridge, Mess Attendant Second Class Doris Miller helped carry the dying Bennion to a safer place. Before rescuing the captain from the flames, Miller, twenty-two, manned a machine gun, which he had never been trained to operate, and fired at the attackers until he was out of ammunition. Like Flaherty, Ward, Tomich, and Reeves, Bennion was posthumously honored with the Medal of Honor. Miller was the first African American to be awarded the Navy Cross.

***Explosion on the* Shaw**
During the second wave of the attack, dive bombers ignited the destroyer *Shaw*'s forward magazines, turning the vessel into an inferno.

Smoke and flames

Departing Japanese planes leave behind the burning hulks of the *Shaw (left)* and the battleship *Nevada (right)*.

Attacking Pearl Harbor

At the launch point for the attack, 230 miles north of Pearl Harbor, the six carriers of Japan's Pearl Harbor strike force readied for takeoff and at dawn turned their bows into the wind. The sky was dark, and the sea was so rough that launching was dangerous, but Commander Mitsuo Fuchida refused to delay the attack.

One by one, the planes in the carrier strike force roared into the sky. The pilots of the attack planes had been meticulously prepared, using a detailed model of the island to study every aspect of their missions. Minoru Genda, operations officer on the flagship carrier *Akagi,* remarked on the effectiveness of this approach. "On the day of the air raid over Oahu Island," he recalled, "it was so cloudy that only a small part of the island was seen. But a pilot [from the *Akagi*] . . . could estimate the location of the coast west of Kaneohe by catching sight of a small patch of land . . . and could immediately choose the right flying course." Oahu, he said, was "just like our model for practice."

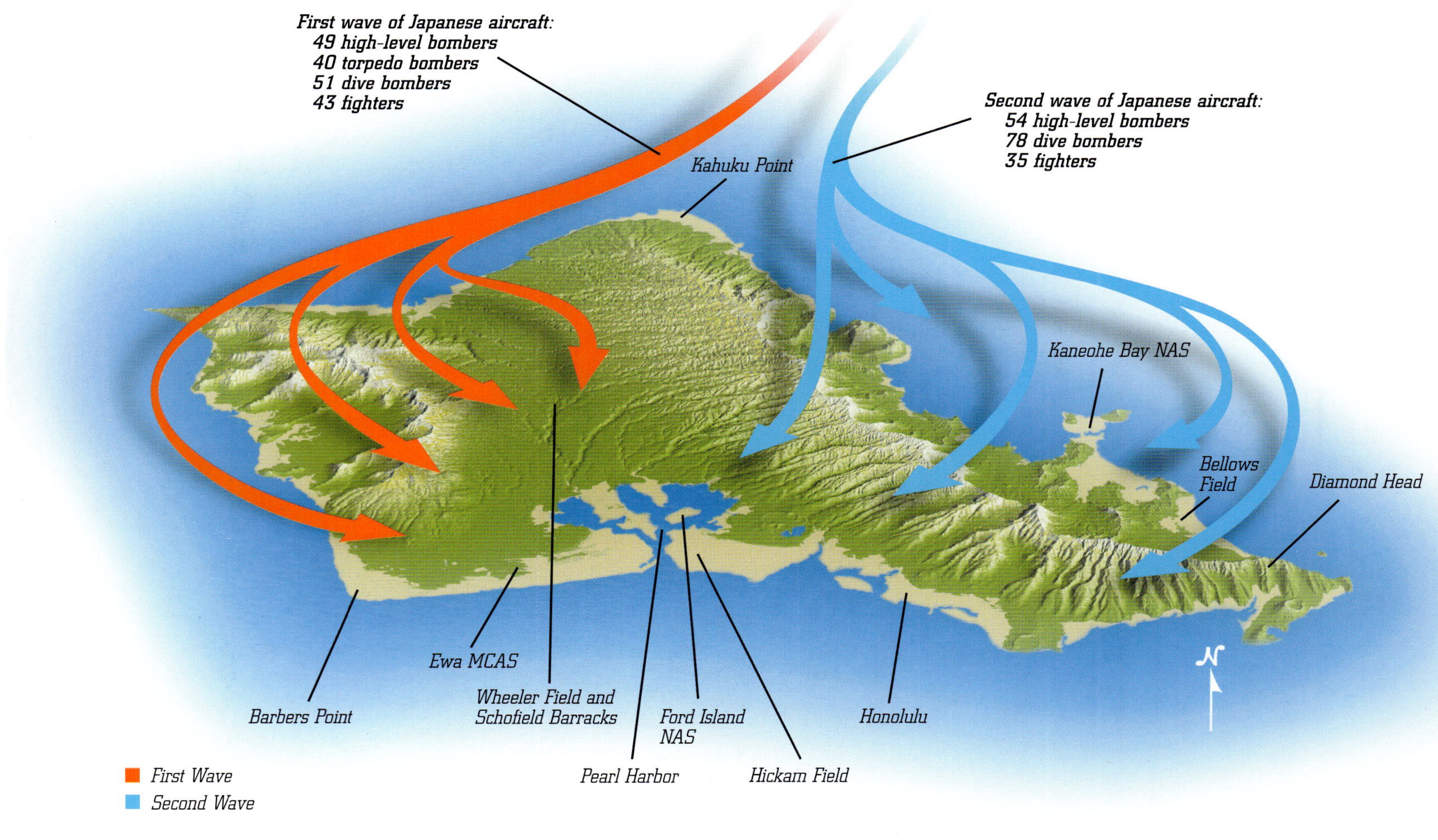

PEARL HARBOR

SECOND WAVE: 8:54 A.M.

As the first wave of Japanese attackers began bombing their targets on Oahu, a second wave of 167 planes was on its way toward the island bases. Launched an hour after the first wave, the second strike force was made up of seventy-eight dive bombers, fifty-four high-level bombers, and thirty-five fighters. Their mission was to complete the destruction of the airfields and target the unhit and lightly damaged warships in the harbor.

By 8:40 A.M., the first wave of attackers was leaving the smoke and wreckage of the island and heading back toward the fleet of aircraft carriers. Japan had lost three fighters, one dive bomber, and five torpedo planes in the first wave. The second wave, led by Lieutenant Commander Shigekazu Shimazaki, approached its targets through columns of smoke and fierce anti-aircraft fire. Sweeping in over the island's eastern shore at 8:54 A.M., the second wave launched its attack.

Kaneohe Bay

First Wave: 7:53 A.M.

Second Wave: 8:55 A.M.

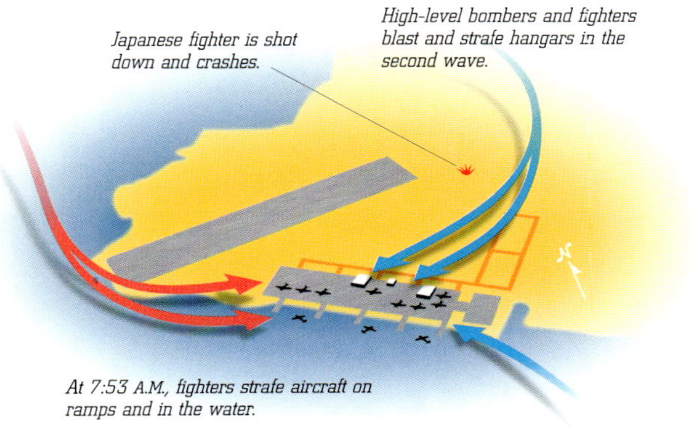

Kaneohe Bay Naval Air Station, on the east side of Oahu, was one of the first air bases to be hit. Home to thirty-six PBY reconnaissance seaplanes, the base contained thirty-three of the flying boats on the morning of the attack. Fighters made strafing runs over the exposed planes, while high-level bombers blasted the hangars. By the time the first- and second-wave attackers flew off, most of the planes and facilities at Kaneohe Bay were burning and badly damaged.

Wheeler Field

First Wave: 7:51 A.M.

Second Wave: 9:10 A.M.

Wheeler Field, near the center of the island, was the U.S. Army's biggest fighter plane base in the Pacific. On the morning of December 7, 140 fighters were parked wingtip to wingtip in the field. At 7:51 A.M., Japanese dive bombers and fighters pounded the exposed fighters, as well as the base's hangars, fuel depot, post exchange, fire station, mess hall, and residences. Within a few minutes, the attackers destroyed much of the airpower protecting the U.S. Pacific Fleet. Fighters returned in strafing runs during the second wave.

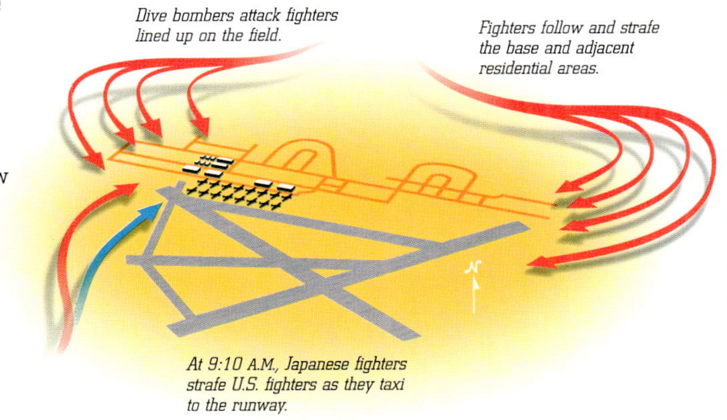

Hickam Field

First Wave: 7:55 A.M.

Second Wave: 9:05 A.M.

Hickam Field housed the 18th Bombardment Wing: twelve B-17s, twelve A-20s, and thirty-three B-18s.

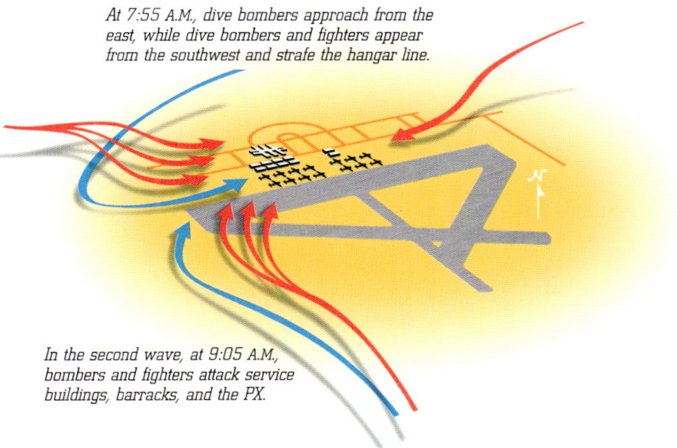

Shortly before 8:00 A.M., dive bombers took aim at Hickam's hangars and flight line, and fighters strafed the parked aircraft. In the middle of the action, twelve unarmed American B-17 bombers flew in from the mainland, attempting to land at Hickam. Attacking fighters shot up two of them. One of the planes flew east with two wounded crew members and crash-landed at Bellows Field; the other burst into flames on the runway at Hickam. During the second wave, twenty-seven high-level bombers ferociously blasted hangars and repair facilities, while fighters strafed crews scrambling on the ground.

PEARL HARBOR
FIRST WAVE: 7:50 A.M.

At 6:15 A.M., the first attack wave of 183 Japanese fighters, bombers, and torpedo planes took off from the carrier decks and set their course due south for Pearl Harbor. At 7:40, the aerial strike force, comprised of forty-three fighters, fifty-one dive bombers, forty-nine high-level bombers, and forty torpedo bombers, sighted the Oahu coast.

After flying over Kahuku Point on the island's northern tip, Commander Mitsuo Fuchida fired a shot from his signal pistol, ordering his torpedo bombers to lead the surprise attack. The fighter planes missed the signal, however, so Fuchida fired again. This time, the fighters saw the shot, but the dive bombers mistook the second signal as an order that they should lead the raid. Despite the confusion as the planes deployed, Fuchida radioed the code to begin the strike. The dive bombers split into two groups: one heading to Ford Island and Hickam Field and the other to Wheeler Field. Encountering no enemy fire, Fuchida radioed a second signal, confirming for the fleet that the attack was a complete surprise.

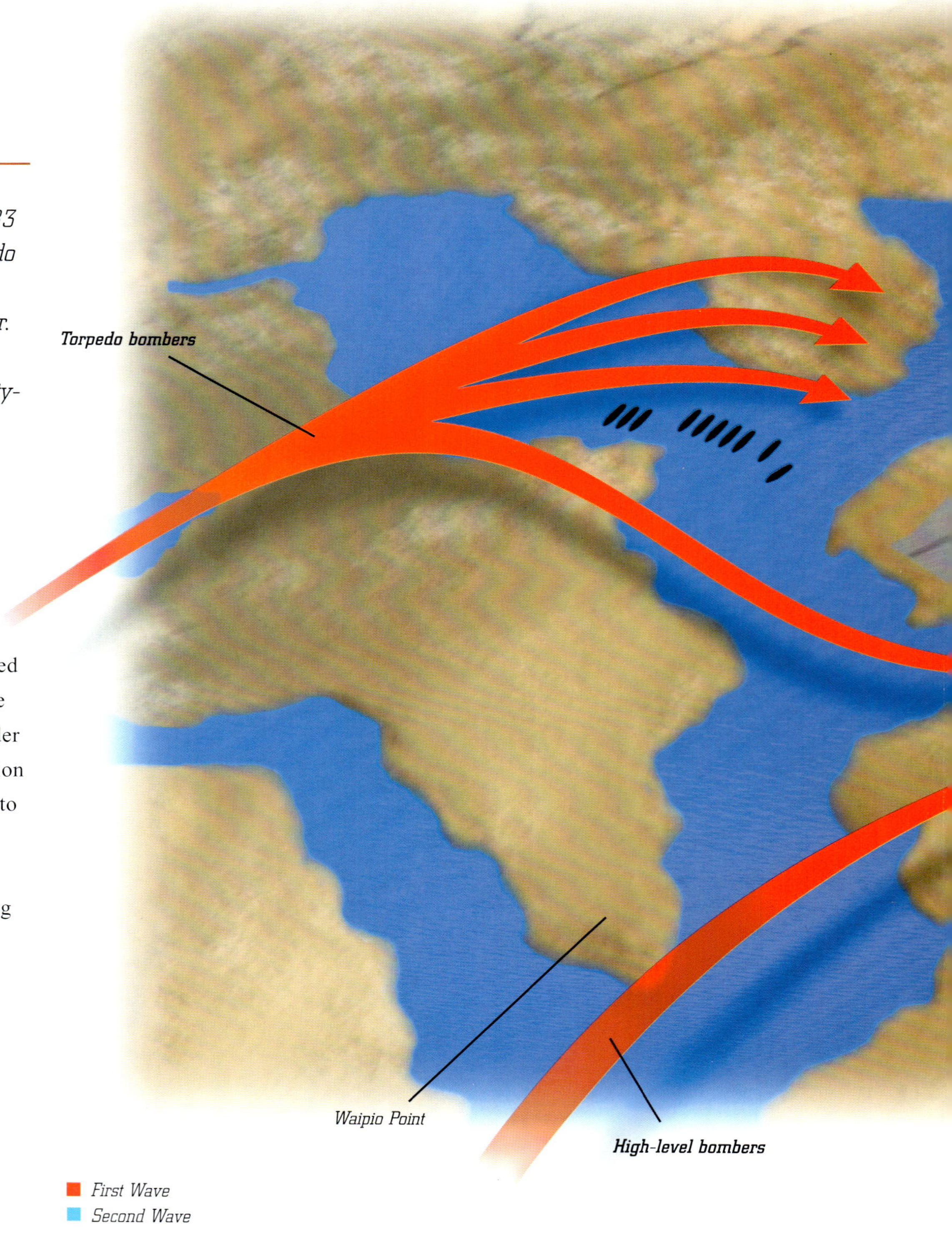

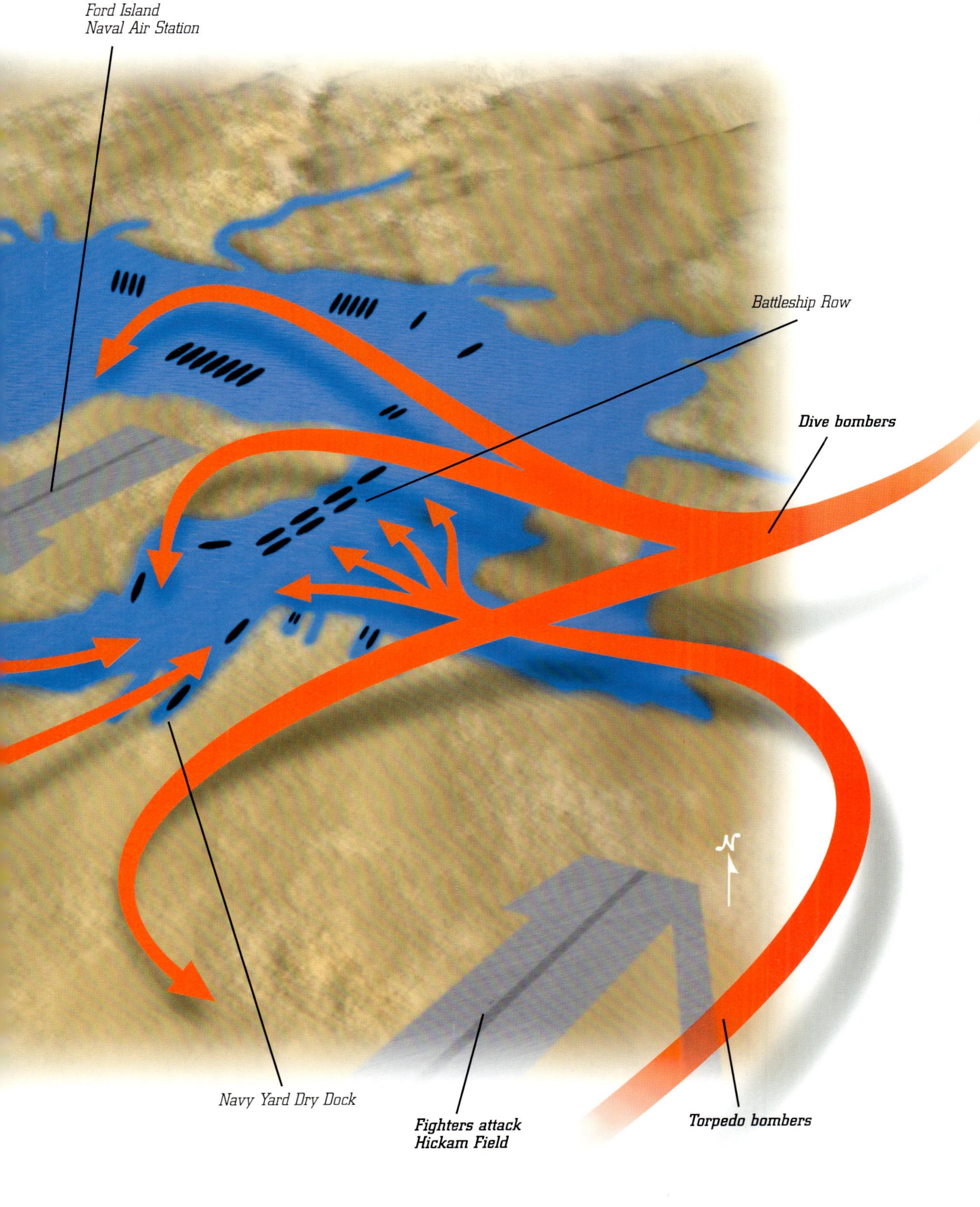

Ford Island NAS

FIRST WAVE: 7:53 A.M.

Nine dive bombers swarmed over Ford Island Naval Air Station, blasting the base's fighters, patrol planes, and hangars as sixteen torpedo planes targeted ships moored on the west side of the island. Two torpedoes hit the target ship, *Utah,* capsizing it and killing fifty-eight sailors. Another torpedo struck the light cruiser *Raleigh,* flooding it and knocking out its power. The light cruiser *Detroit* and seaplane tender *Tangier* escaped damage. The fighters also hit two ships berthed together at the Navy Yard, the minelayer *Oglala* and the light cruiser *Helena*. A torpedo exploded against the *Helena*'s side, damaging both ships and causing the *Oglala* to capsize.

At the same time, twenty-four torpedo bombers and forty-nine high-level bombers attacked Battleship Row on the east side of Ford Island. Direct bomb hits destroyed the *Arizona,* killing 1,177 men. Torpedoes and bombs blasted the *West Virginia,* sinking her upright in the harbor. Two bombs struck the *Tennessee* and the repair ship *Vestal,* while nine torpedoes tore into the *Oklahoma,* capsizing her and killing 415 sailors. The *Nevada* took one torpedo hit before getting underway, and three torpedo blasts flooded the *California*.

Bellows Field

First Wave: 8:30 A.M.

Second Wave: 9:00 A.M.

Bellows Field, located near Kaneohe Bay Naval Air Station, was home to nine O-47 observation planes and twelve P-40 fighters. Although Bellows had been strafed with little damage during the first wave of the attack, in the second wave the airfield was not spared. At 9:00 A.M., eight fighters strafed parked planes and a few that were trying to take off. Two pilots managed to get their aircraft off the ground, but they were quickly shot down by the attackers.

In the first-wave attack, at 8:30 A.M., a single fighter strafes tents and buildings near the runway.

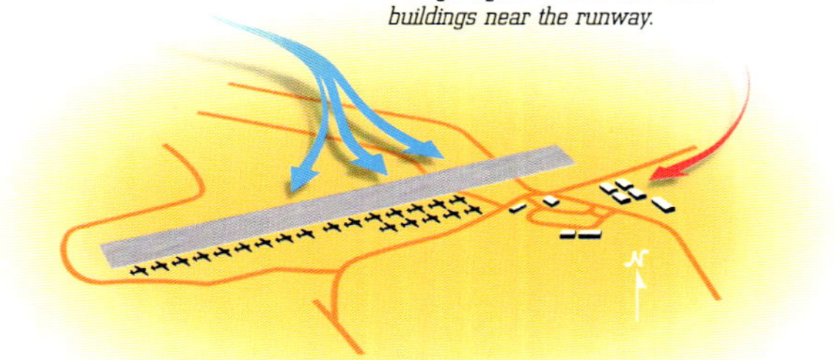

In the second wave at 9:00 A.M., fighters attack parked aircraft.

Ewa MCAS

First Wave: 7:53 A.M.

Second Wave: 9:10 A.M.

In the first wave, at 7:53 A.M., fighters strafe aircraft on runway.

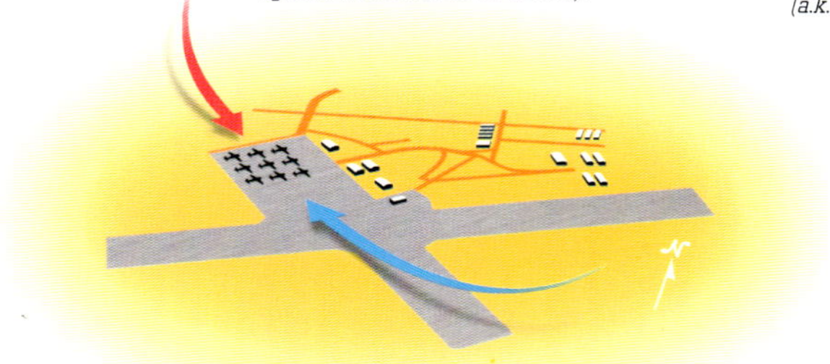

In the second wave, between 9:10 and 9:45 A.M., a small group of fighters and dive bombers, following their attack on Hickam Field and Kaneohe Bay, strafe planes at Ewa.

Ewa Marine Corps Air Station, outside Pearl Harbor, was pounded by fighters and dive bombers in both waves of the raid. As the attackers' last stop before leaving Oahu, the marine base took a heavy beating. Although marines fired back with machine guns during the second wave, the toll was heavy. Four men were killed, and thirty-three of the base's forty-eight planes were destroyed or damaged.

Second-wave attackers

The second-wave strike involved no torpedo planes. Instead, it relied on Japan's fastest and most maneuverable aircraft: dive bombers, fighters, and high-level bombers. Fighters were lightweight, aggressive, and powerfully armed with four machine guns. The dive bombers each carried a 550-pound bomb, and the high-level bombers were loaded with 550- or 125-pound bombs.

Dive Bomber (a.k.a. Val)

Fighter (a.k.a. Zero)

Torpedo Bomber (a.k.a. Kate)

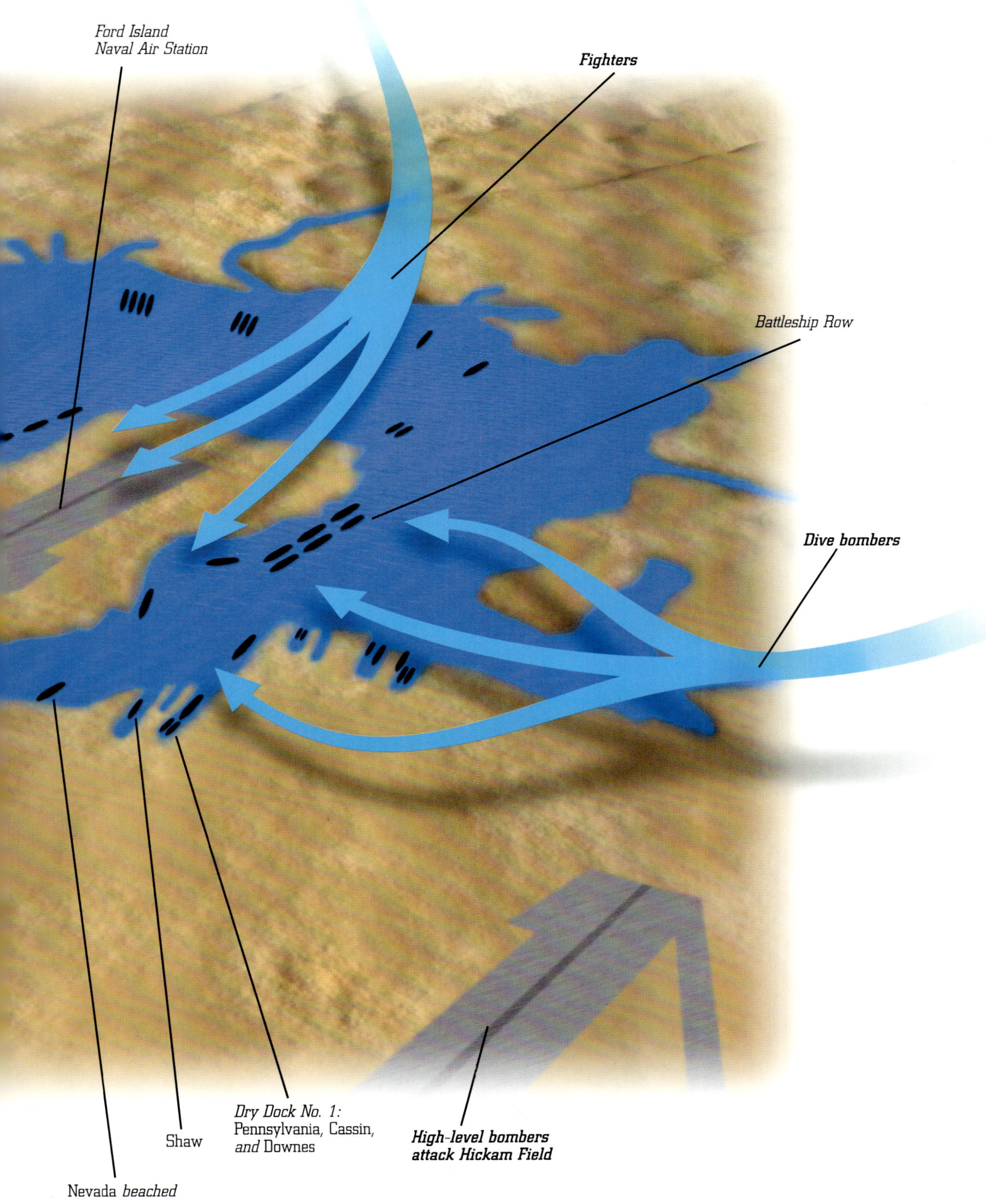

Ford Island NAS

Second Wave: 9:02 A.M.

Dive bombers, fighters, and high-level bombers converged on Ford Island and Battleship Row. The damaged battleship *Nevada* was now making its way into the main channel of the harbor, and twenty-three dive bombers pounded her with furious attacks. Blasting the *Nevada* with five direct bomb hits, the Japanese planes attempted to sink the vessel and block the narrow entrance of the harbor. The *Nevada*'s crew, however, was able to beach the warship opposite Ford Island.

With smoke obscuring targets in the harbor, a squadron of dive bombers headed for the Pearl Harbor Navy Yard. At 9:07 A.M., a bomb hit the battleship *Pennsylvania* in Dry Dock No. 1, killing fifteen seamen. The destroyers *Cassin* and *Downes,* next to each other in the dry dock, were struck by bombs that ruptured fuel tanks and set the ships ablaze, causing the *Cassin* to topple over on the *Downes*. Three bombs hit the destroyer *Shaw,* in floating Dry Dock No. 2. Fire ignited by the third blast later exploded the vessel's forward magazines, engulfing the *Shaw* in a massive fireball.

Target Pearl Harbor

A Japanese fighter flies over the Pearl Harbor Navy Yard.

It was 1:35 P.M. in Washington, D.C.—ten minutes after bombs began falling in Hawaii—when the president heard the news, by telephone, from Secretary of the Navy Frank Knox. A Honolulu alert message, "AIR RAID ON PEARL HARBOR—THIS IS NOT DRILL," had been picked up by navy communications. Harry Hopkins, meeting with the president in his study, was certain that there had to be some mistake, but Roosevelt suspected that the report "was perfectly true." For days, the president had been worrying about how to win public support for American military action in the Pacific. Now, before learning any details of the destruction in Hawaii, President Roosevelt seemed calm, even relieved. The Japanese, he told Hopkins, had "made the decision for him"; the matter, at last, was out of his hands.

AFTERMATH

The news of the surprise attack "fell like a bombshell in Washington," the *New York Times* reported, climaxing a day of heightening alarm. Ominous signs of a major diplomatic and military Japanese move had been apparent since early that morning. Just after 5:00 A.M., the long-awaited fourteenth part of the Japanese reply had finally been intercepted. Decoded and translated, the dispatch was waiting for Lieutenant Commander Alwin D. Kramer of Naval Intelligence when he arrived at his office at 7:30 A.M. This time, Tokyo's wording was blunt: ". . . the earnest hope of the Japanese government . . . to preserve and promote the peace of the Pacific through cooperation with the American government has finally been lost . . . it is impossible to reach an agreement through further negotiations."

Black day

Dark plumes of smoke from Battleship Row, *left,* loom over shops and ammunition storage buildings at Pearl Harbor. A navy dispatch from the Commander in Chief Pacific (CINCPAC) at Pearl Harbor, *right,* disclosed the first news of Japan's surprise attack on the Hawaiian base.

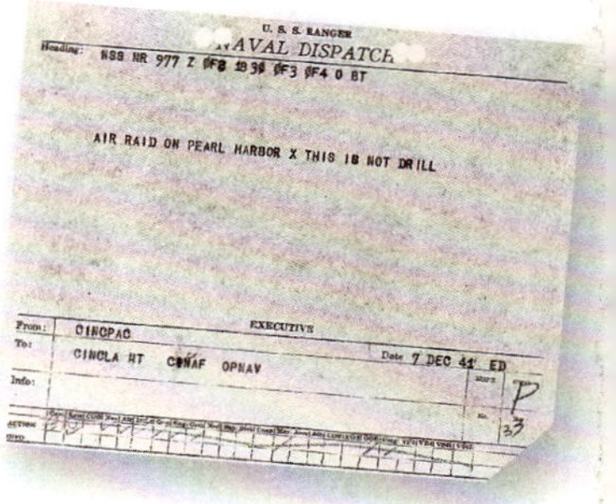

U. S. S. RANGER
NAVAL DISPATCH
Heading: NSS NR 977 Z ØF8 1830 ØF3 ØF4 0 BT

AIR RAID ON PEARL HARBOR X THIS IS NOT DRILL

From: CINCPAC
EXECUTIVE
To: CINCLA NT CONAF OPNAV
Date 7 DEC 41 ED
Info:

Kramer quickly took the dispatch to Commander A. H. McCollum, chief of Naval Intelligence's Far Eastern Section, then set off to deliver copies at around 9:30 A.M.—first to Admiral Stark, then to the White House and the State Department. At the same time, Colonel Rufus Bratton, chief of the army's Far Eastern Section, was urgently trying to reach General George C. Marshall, who did not yet know about the first thirteen sections of the message. Marshall was horseback riding in the Virginia woods; when he finally phoned into the War Department, it was nearly 10:30 A.M. By that time, yet another Japanese dispatch had been intercepted, decoded, and translated. It read: "Will the ambassador please submit to the

United States Government (if possible to the Secretary of State) our reply to the United States at 1:00 P.M. on the 7th, your time." The dispatch, known as the "one o'clock message," stunned Bratton; the Asian specialist was convinced that it meant "the Japanese were going to attack some American installation in the Pacific area"—although, he recalled later, it never occurred to him that Pearl Harbor would be the target.

Returning to the Navy Department, Kramer, too, saw the one o'clock message, along with other cables instructing the Japanese embassy in Washington to destroy its codes. Kramer quickly calculated that 1:00 P.M. in Washington would be 7:30 A.M. in Hawaii, "probably the quietest time of the week aboard ship at Pearl Harbor," he noted. More significantly, he thought, it would be a few hours before dawn in Thailand and Malaya, prime time for an amphibious attack. Rushing to Admiral Stark's office, he gave the documents to McCollum, pointing out the timing of the message. Kramer and McCollum both believed, like Bratton, that the one o'clock message signaled a Japanese attack on Thailand or the Malay Peninsula; neither considered or discussed the possibility that Japan's target would be Hawaii.

When General Marshall finally arrived at the War Department and read the intercepted messages, it was nearly

Ruin and wreckage

Debris from a P-40 fighter plane, a twin-engine amphibian, and a blasted hangar, *right,* litter an army airfield. After the attack, the maintenance hangars were bombed out, recalled Lieutenant Everett Stewart, and there were burned airplanes up and down the flight line. "It looks like we've had it for now," Stewart thought to himself. "They got us."

Secretary Hull

Secretary of State Cordell Hull, *below (right),* confers with Representative Sol Bloom, chairman of the Foreign Affairs Committee. Hull's grave face was "as white as his hair" when he arrived at the White House the afternoon of the attack, recalled the president's personal secretary, Grace Tully.

11:30 A.M. He, too, concluded that the Japanese were planning to strike somewhere in the Pacific by 1:00 P.M.—a deadline, he realized, that was now only ninety minutes away. After deciding to alert his army commanders, Marshall phoned Admiral Stark, asking if he wanted to warn navy commanders in the Pacific. Stark, according to McCollum, "said he didn't think any further warning was necessary, that they'd had ample warning and he couldn't see it would do any good." On his own, then, Marshall started drafting an alert for Lieutenant General Short on Oahu and General Douglas MacArthur in the Philippines. Before he finished, Stark phoned back, requesting that Marshall add the words "tell navy" to his message.

At 12:00 noon on Sunday, December 7—6:30 A.M. in Honolulu—the Army Signal Corps filed Marshall's handwritten warning: "Japanese are presenting at 1 pm eastern standard time today what amounts to an ultimatum also they are under orders to destroy their code machine immediately. Just what significance the hour set may have we do not know but be on the alert accordingly. Inform naval authorities of this communication." Some fifteen minutes later, the warning was transmitted by commercial Western Union telegram to the RCA offices in Honolulu. From there, Marshall's dispatch was handed to a Honolulu motorcycle messenger, who was instructed to deliver it to Short at Fort Shafter. Nothing on the envelope indicated that the telegram inside was urgent. It was now 7:40 A.M. Hawaii time—only fifteen minutes before the bombs began to fall.

News of the attack

Western Union messengers race out of the White House on December 7, 1941. President Roosevelt ordered war bulletins released as soon as news came in of the Pearl Harbor attack.

At the White House, the atmosphere was calm, despite the troubling cables from Japan. At 12:30 P.M., Roosevelt met with China's ambassador, Dr. Hu Shih, and read him his letter to the Japan's emperor "with an air of leisure and gusto," the ambassador recalled. "This is my last effort for peace. I am afraid," the president added, "that it may fail." Within forty-eight hours, Roosevelt predicted, the Japanese might do something "nasty" in Thailand, the Dutch East Indies, Malaya, and "possibly" the Philippines. Secretary of War Henry L. Stimson, too, felt sure that the Japanese were planning to strike soon. "Today is the day," Stimson wrote in his diary that morning, "that the Japanese are going to bring their answer to Hull, and everything in Magic indicated they had been keeping the time back until now in order to accomplish something hanging in the air." He wrote later that the president phoned him at 2:00 P.M. "Have you heard the news?" Roosevelt asked in a "rather excited" voice. Stimson replied, "Well, I have heard the telegrams which have been coming in about the Japanese advances in the Gulf of Siam." "Oh, no, I don't mean that," the president told him. "They have attacked Hawaii. They are now bombing Hawaii."

Roosevelt also telephoned news of the attack to Secretary Hull at the State Department, where Nomura and Kurusu had just arrived.

The diplomats had postponed their planned 1:00 P.M. meeting with Hull for an hour because of embassy delays in preparing the fourteen-part message from Tokyo. Roosevelt advised Hull simply to read the message they presented and dismiss them. At 2:20 P.M., Hull received the envoys and coldly kept them standing while he scanned the document. Then, glaring at Nomura, he declared, "I have never seen a document that was more crowded with . . . infamous falsehoods and distortions on a scale so huge that I never imagined until today that any government on this planet was capable of uttering them." He then motioned abruptly for the diplomats to leave his office.

At that very moment, Japanese bombers were streaking over Pearl Harbor, blasting planes and ships into flaming wrecks. In utter disbelief, completely stunned, Admiral Kimmel had watched the first moments of the catastrophe from his home above Battleship Row, his face as pale as his white navy uniform. It was not until 3:00 P.M.—some five hours after the attack—that an army courier finally brought him General Marshall's warning, filed eight and a half hours earlier. The motorcycle messenger, held up by huge traffic jams, had not delivered the message to Fort Shafter until shortly before noon; it was nearly 3:00 P.M. before the warning was at last decoded and given to Short. Kimmel tossed the message in the trash, stating that it was no longer of any interest to him at all.

White House meeting

On the night of December 7, members of Congress, including Senator Thomas T. Connally (D-Texas), *below,* chairman of the Foreign Relations Committee, gather at the White House to confer with the president and members of the cabinet. "I am amazed by the attack by Japan, but I am still more astounded at what happened to our navy. They were all asleep," Connally angrily remarked after listening to Roosevelt's account of the attack.

Now, navigating the burning wreckage of the harbor, the flotilla of small boats and life rafts was continuing to pull injured and burned sailors out of the water and carry them to refuge on Ford Island. Some survivors, black with oil, their skin charred and red with bloody wounds, managed to crawl up onto the island from the water; many lay down and died there on its grassy banks. Those among the wounded who could still walk streamed into the naval officers' quarters on the island, where the uninjured tried to make them comfortable without medical help. Volunteers collected cots, bedding, underwear, shirts, uniforms, shoes, and socks, while others handed out cigarettes, candy bars, and water to thousands of wounded men. They "kept streaming in, crowding up to the counter," recalled Betty Garrett, one of the volunteers. She had to light cigarettes and hold cups of water for many of the men because their hands were shaking so violently. By now, hospitals on Oahu were overflowing with casualties. At Schofield Barracks Army Hospital, "they were bringing men in so quickly that they didn't have time to separate the living from the dead," remembered army nurse Myrtle Watson. Wounded men were lining the halls on litters that were soaked with blood; a nurse was going down the line, giving them all shots of morphine and marking red "Ms" on their foreheads to show that they had been medicated. Men who had been terribly burned, their skin black and oozing, lay in pain under hooped sheets.

Out of the blue

Stunned by the attack, Joe Ciampi from Ocala, Florida, takes a break with other armed marines on the parade grounds, wondering if the surprise strike force will return.

"Basins were placed beneath the beds to catch the blood that soaked through the thin hospital mattresses," Watson recalled. "No one speaks," First Lieutenant Cornelius C. Smith Jr. wrote in his diary. "Few can even move, but pathetic eyes follow me as I go through the wards. These men look so young, just kids, some of them."

In Honolulu, calls had gone out over the radio for doctors, nurses, and defense workers to report for emergency duty. There were casualties within the city, too. Honolulu was damaged by American anti-aircraft shells, which killed forty-eight civilians. Early that morning, many residents had seen the Japanese planes fly in over the island, some skimming so low that it seemed as if they would graze the rooftops. Sixteen-year-old Rose Mary Souza and her brother had climbed up onto their roof to watch the planes fly by. Thinking the pilots were American, "we waved our arms at them," Souza recalled, and some of the planes responded by tipping their wings. It was not until 8:40 A.M. that the radio began reporting the frightening reality of the strike: "A sporadic air attack has been made on Oahu . . . enemy planes have been shot down . . . the rising sun has been sighted on the wingtips." Finally, at about 9:00 A.M., radio broadcaster Webley Edwards began announcing, over and over again: "Attention. This is no exercise. This is the real McCoy! The Japanese are attacking Pearl Harbor!" Sometime later, remembered Esther Oyer Hoag, Edwards broadcast America's national anthem, warning his radio listeners that they might never hear it again.

Late that afternoon in Pearl Harbor, two navy officers, ensigns Kleber S. Masterson and Jim Dare, took a motor launch over to the *Arizona* and went aboard the vessel—"what was left of it," Masterson recalled. At sunset, they hauled down the American flag, "the big Sunday ensign flying from the stern" that was now dragging in the oil-slicked water of the harbor. Others, too, had returned to the wrecked ships. Commander Lorenzo S. Seton inspected the *Nevada* with Rear Admiral Walter S. Anderson. "We saw a scene of complete shambles," Seton remembered. "The grim effects of her punishment were everywhere," especially on the main deck, topside, and the upper structure. The ship's decks and bulkheads were red with blood; "twisted masses of metal and spidery steel were spattered with blood, while bodies and parts of bodies were being pulled from the debris." On the *Tennessee,* remembered seaman Jack Kelley, crewmen went aboard with mattress covers to recover all the pieces of human flesh. Meanwhile, soldiers had gathered at mass graves on the island,

Aiding the wounded

A serviceman, *right,* assists one of the wounded after the attack. The island's hospitals were packed with casualties, and schools were turned into makeshift wards to receive and care for all the wounded. The days following the raid, recalled an army nurse, were "a blur of activity: nursing the dying, giving them whiskey and morphine, eating only chocolate bars and coffee, worrying about a Japanese invasion, little sleep, blood, death, and more blood."

Fliers on film

Replicas of Japanese war planes, *below,* attack Oahu in the 1970 film *Tora! Tora! Tora!*

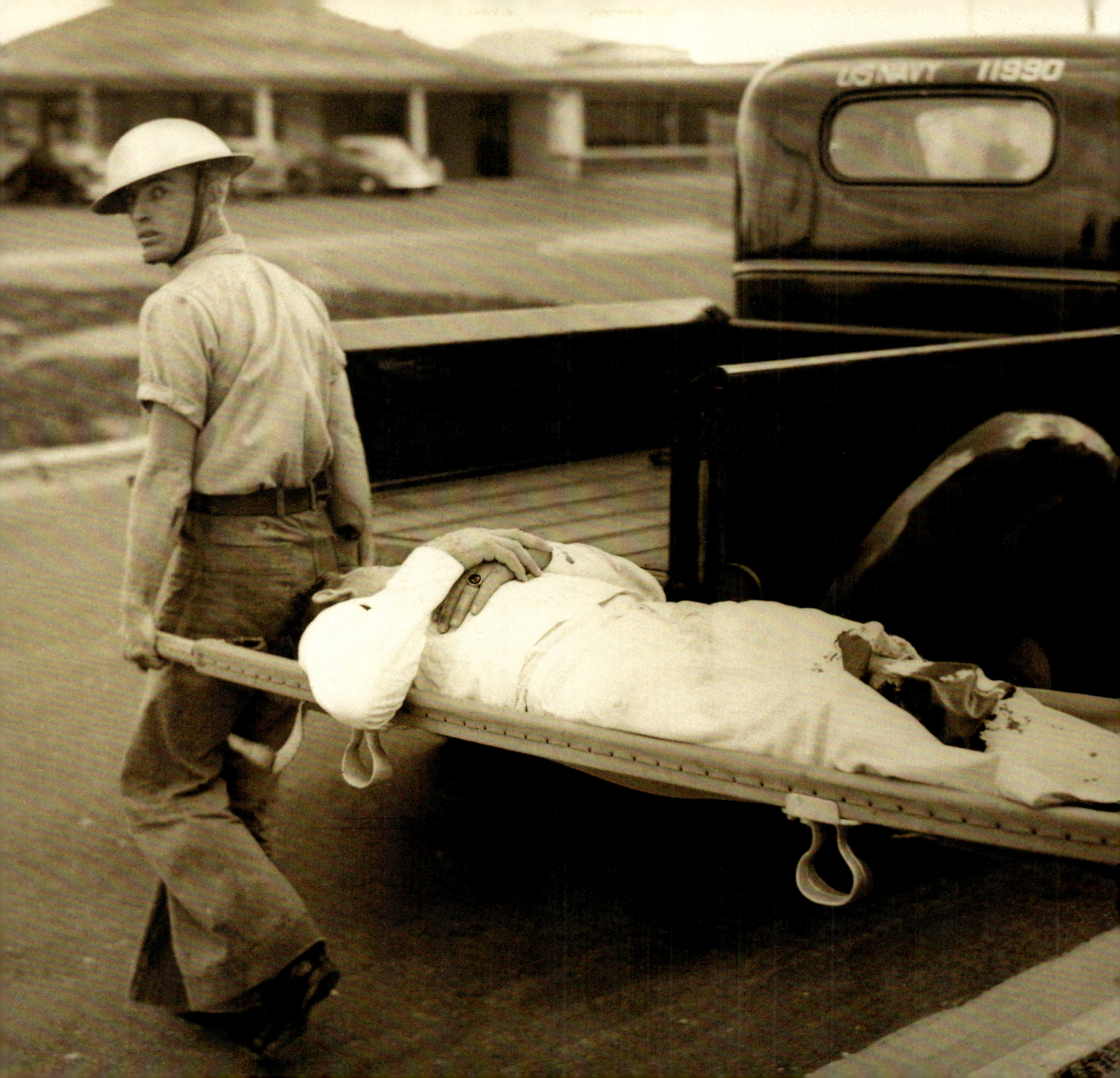
US NAVY 11990

bulldozing trenches 150 feet long to receive the bodies and remains of all the dead. Hundreds of crude, makeshift wooden boxes, many of them leaking blood and oil, were given whatever identification was possible and placed, side by side, into the ground.

That night, on Oahu, there was little sleep. Catastrophic rumors spread everywhere—that Japanese parachutists and snipers were on the island, that the Japanese fleet was offshore within firing range, that Honolulu was burning, that the island's water supply had been poisoned by saboteurs. "It was the longest, the darkest, and the wildest night that I can recall," remembered Ted T. Tsukiyama. Shocked and disoriented, fearful of another attack, armed servicemen were shooting at anything suspicious, and anti-aircraft fire lit up Pearl Harbor "like a carousel." A patrol plane killed four fishermen returning to the island with their catch. Wild fire shot down a civilian plane, and six fighter planes from the carrier *Enterprise*, ordered to land on Oahu, flew straight into a deadly anti-aircraft barrage. Betty Garrett remembered people "cheering wildly as our gunners opened fire on planes flying overhead," followed by an anguished hush when the crowd learned that the gunners had shot down American planes.

Destroyed B-17

A B-17 bomber, burnt after taking a hit from a Japanese gunner, lies on the runway at, Hickam Field. At about 8:20 A.M. on December 7, twelve B-17s en route from California to Oahu flew right into the middle of the attack. Unarmed and low on fuel, the planes became instant prey for Japanese fighters.

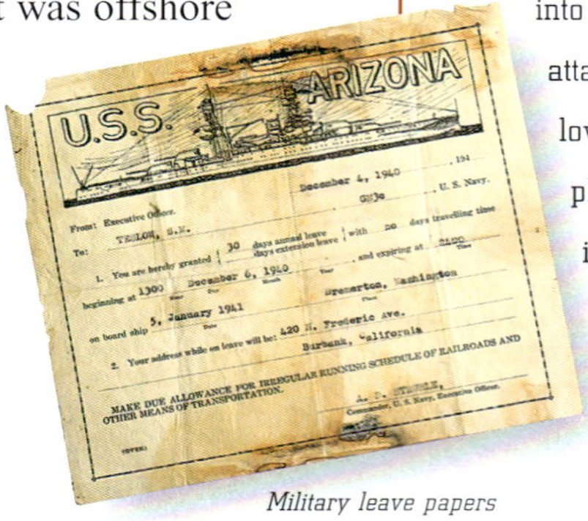

U.S.S. ARIZONA

December 4, 1940, 194

U. S. Navy.

From: Executive Officer.

To: TEILOR, S.M.

1. You are hereby granted 30 days annual leave / days extension leave with no days travelling time beginning at 1300 December 6, 1940 and expiring at 2400 on board ship 5, January 1941 Bremerton, Washington

2. Your address while on leave will be: 420 N. Frederic Ave. Burbank, California

MAKE DUE ALLOWANCE FOR IRREGULAR RUNNING SCHEDULE OF RAILROADS AND OTHER MEANS OF TRANSPORTATION.

Commander, U. S. Navy, Executive Officer.

(OVER)

Military leave papers

In Washington, the details of the disaster had come in piecemeal throughout the day. The news from Hawaii, Stimson recorded, "is very bad. . . . It has been staggering to see our people there, who have been warned long ago and were standing on the alert, should have been so caught by surprise." The lack of preparedness was "just unexplainable," Treasury Secretary Henry Morgenthau stated. Roosevelt, increasingly tense, shaken, and angry, had received scattered accounts of the attack all day as he worked in his study, while outside the White House crowds of citizens gathered, some singing "God Bless America." At 8:30 P.M., members of the cabinet arrived and assembled in Roosevelt's study, now crammed with extra chairs and maps. "We just got scraps of information," recalled Secretary of Labor Frances Perkins; "nobody knew exactly what had happened . . . where the planes had come from." Roosevelt, who had always been so proud of the navy, "was having actual physical difficulty in getting out the words that bombs dropped on ships" that were just tied up in harbor. Members of Congress were soon filling the study, and the president briefed them on the few details he had of the attack. Whether he would ask Congress for a declaration of war was not yet clear; the president "didn't say," Speaker of the House Sam Rayburn told a reporter as he left the White House. Nevertheless, events were quickly moving forward. At 4:00 P.M. Washington time, Japan had issued a formal declaration of war on the United States and the British Empire. Japan, "for its existence and self-defense, has no other recourse," Emperor Hirohito proclaimed, "but to appeal to arms and to crush every obstacle in its path."

The next day, draped in his old navy cape, Roosevelt went to the House Chamber to appear before a joint session of Congress. The mood in the chamber was grim, tense, and determined. "Everybody knew that we were in for something terrible," Perkins recalled. "We had all been trained to think of the United States as invincible, and now we were faced with the fact that our navy had cracked." The president, looking tired and drawn, solemnly asked Congress to declare "that, since the unprovoked and dastardly attack by Japan on Sunday, December 7, a state of war has existed between the United States and the Japanese Empire."

White House vigil
Anxious crowds of people, bundled against the chill, assembled on Pennsylvania Avenue outside the White House gates on the afternoon and evening of December 7. Cheering as streams of limousines arrived, delivering the cabinet and members of congress to the White House, many sang patriotic songs as the lights inside the mansion burned late into the night.

President Roosevelt's War Address

Delivered to a Joint Session of Congress on Monday, December 8, 1941, at 12:30 P.M.

Yesterday, December 7, 1941—a date which will live in infamy—the United States of America was suddenly and deliberately attacked by naval and air forces of the Empire of Japan.

The United States was at peace with that nation and, at the solicitation of Japan, was still in conversation with its Government and its Emperor looking toward the maintenance of peace in the Pacific. Indeed, one hour after Japanese air squadrons had commenced bombing Oahu, the Japanese Ambassador to the United States [Kichisaburo Nomura] and his colleague [Saburo Kurusu] delivered to the Secretary of State a formal reply to a recent American message. While this reply stated that it seemed useless to continue the existing diplomatic negotiations, it contained no threat or hint of war or armed attack.

It will be recorded that the distance of Hawaii from Japan makes it obvious that the attack was deliberately planned many days or even weeks ago.

During the intervening time, the Japanese Government has deliberately sought to deceive the United States by false statements and expressions of hope for continued peace.

*The attack yesterday on the Hawaiian Islands has caused severe damage to American naval and military forces. Very many American lives have been lost. In addition, American ships have been reported torpedoed on the high seas between San Francisco and Honolulu.**

Yesterday the Japanese Government also launched an attack against Malaya.

Last night Japanese forces attacked Hong Kong.

Last night Japanese forces attacked Guam.

Last night Japanese forces attacked the Philippine Islands.

America declares war

The day after the Pearl Harbor attack, President Roosevelt, *far left,* asked Congress for a declaration of war. The joint resolution adopted by Congress and signed at 4:10 P.M. on December 8, decreed that "a state of war between the United States and the Imperial government of Japan is hereby formally declared; and the president is hereby authorized and directed to employ the entire naval and military forces of the United States and the resources of the government to carry on war against the Imperial government of Japan; and, to bring the conflict to a successful termination, all of the resources of the country are hereby pledged by the Congress of the United States." Three days later, on December 11, Roosevelt, *left,* signed Congress's declaration of war against Germany and Italy.

Last night the Japanese attacked Wake Island.

This morning the Japanese attacked Midway Island.

Japan has therefore undertaken a surprise offensive extending throughout the Pacific area. The facts of yesterday speak for themselves. The people of the United States have already formed their opinions and well understand the implications to the very life and safety of our nation.

As Commander in Chief of the Army and Navy I have directed that all measures be taken for our defense.

Always will we remember the character of the onslaught against us.

No matter how long it may take us to overcome this premeditated invasion, the American people in their righteous might will win through to absolute victory.

I believe I interpret the will of the Congress and of the people when I assert that we will not only defend ourselves to the uttermost but will make very certain that this form of treachery shall never endanger us again.

Hostilities exist. There is no blinking at the fact that our people, our territory, and our interests are in grave danger.

With confidence in our armed forces—with the unbounded determination of our people—we will gain the inevitable triumph, so help us God.

I ask that the Congress declare that, since the unprovoked and dastardly attack by Japan on Sunday, December 7, a state of war has existed between the United States and the Japanese Empire.

* These reports were inaccurate.

The chamber erupted in thunderous cheers and applause, an expression, Perkins observed, "of men trying to say, 'We stand with you.'" Thirty-three minutes later, Congress approved the resolution, with just one dissenting vote.

In Berlin, Hitler reacted joyfully when he learned of the Pearl Harbor attack. After a press officer brought him the news, the Führer slapped his thighs and exclaimed, "The turning point!" Now that Japan had attacked America, he predicted, "it is impossible for us to lose the war." In Japan, Germany had "an ally who has never been vanquished in three thousand years"; in Italy, he asserted, his nation had another ally "who has constantly been vanquished but has always ended up on the right side." Mussolini, too, was gratified by news of the attack, according to Count Galeazzo Ciano, Italy's minister of foreign affairs. For a long time, Ciano noted, Mussolini had "been in favor of clarifying the position between America and the Axis." The Tripartite Pact bound Germany, Italy, and Japan to go to war only if one of them was attacked by a third party. In this case, Japan had struck first at the United States, but that did not deter Germany and Italy from declaring war on the United States on December 11. As Hitler explained to dinner companions five months later, Japan's strike at Pearl Harbor came "when the surprises of the Russian winter were pressing most heavily on the morale of our people, and when everybody in Germany was oppressed by the certainty that, sooner or later, the United States would come into the conflict. Japanese intervention," the

End of peace

Trading stops on the floor of the New York Stock Exchange, *left,* as members listen to the broadcast of President Roosevelt's speech to the joint session of Congress. Wall Street stocks sank the day after the Pearl Harbor attack, then shot up to new highs two days later, as industry shifted to a war footing. Leaders of organized labor pledged support for increased production. Citizens steeled themselves for higher taxes as well as for shortages of oil, rubber, and metal, resources that now needed to be conserved for defense purposes. "There would be no leadfoil around candy and cigarettes," one journalist predicted. "Tin cans would have less tin," he warned, and "bathroom plumbing would sparkle with less chrome."

The New York Times.
JAPAN WARS ON U.S. AND BRITAIN; MAKES SUDDEN ATTACK ON HAWAII; HEAVY FIGHTING AT SEA REPORTED

AURORA SUNDAY BEACON-NEWS
U. S.–JAPAN AT WAR!
America Repulses Air-Sea Attack
JAP PLANES KILL 350, SET FIRE TO WARSHIP OKLAHOMA
TOKYO RAIDS PEARL HARBOR NAVAL BASE, THEN DECLARES WAR; ALL U.S. TROOPS CALLED
WAR BULLETINS

Führer judged, "therefore, was, from our point of view, most opportune."

The United States, no longer neutral, was now at war and in it "all the way," Roosevelt told the country in a radio address. "Not only must the shame of Japanese treachery be wiped out," he declared, "but the sources of international brutality, wherever they exist, must be absolutely and finally broken." To meet the new demands of war, he urged that industrial production be accelerated to seven days a week and new capacity be added quickly. Unified by the Pearl Harbor attack, Americans were now steeled and determined to win the war. So many citizens enlisted after the attack that military recruiting stations kept their doors open day and night. By the end of the war, more than 15 million men and women were serving in the armed forces. The civilian labor force had grown from 47 million to 53 million workers, and by 1943, U.S. factories were outproducing those of all the Axis countries combined. Despite the devastating success of Japan's surprise attack, "I fear," Admiral Yamamoto is said to have predicted, that "we have only awakened a sleeping giant and filled him with terrible resolve."

At Pearl Harbor, in the days after the attack, survivors continued to focus on the grim work of recovery. Medical teams, short of critical supplies

including blood, surgical masks, rubber gloves, and operating gowns, struggled to save lives. Crews were working desperately in the harbor to free men who were trapped alive inside the capsized ships. On the *Oklahoma,* Julio de Castro, a civilian navy yard crewman, led a crew that "worked all around the clock," recalled navy yard worker Ernest Pacheco, ". . . drilling and getting that hull open so they could drop down inside the ship." By Tuesday afternoon, de Castro's team had rescued thirty-two men from the upturned battleship, where more than four hundred others had perished.

Recovering from disaster

Repair crews crowd the deck of the *Maryland, above (left),* while rescuers in small boats search for survivors near the burning *West Virginia* and the capsized hull of the *Oklahoma.*

Eyeglasses and case recovered from the USS Arizona

The task of accounting for the dead also continued; for many, it was a terrible duty. Crews struggled to recover bodies from the roasted hulks of ships and the harbor water. Musician Warren G. Harding was assigned to a recovery crew on the *California,* where he discovered that a torpedo had hit the fuel supply. "The people . . . there were literally boiled in oil," Harding remembered; he and the crew could only get them out in pieces. Others, working from small motor boats, lassoed bodies and parts of bodies that floated to the surface, towing them slowly behind motor launches to the shore. There, hospital corpsmen laid the remains of the dead out "like cordwood," Seaman First Class Nick L. Kouretas recalled.

The Roberts Commission

The First Pearl Harbor Investigation

On December 18, 1941, less than two weeks after the Pearl Harbor attack, President Roosevelt appointed a commission to investigate the facts of the disaster and to judge whether there had been dereliction of duty on the part of any army or navy personnel. From December 22, 1941, until January 9, 1942, the five-man board held hearings in Hawaii, taking the testimony of 127 witnesses.

Chaired by Associate Supreme Court Justice Owen J. Roberts, the commission was instructed to observe secrecy and make a "searching investigation" of the attack. Its members included Rear Admiral Joseph M. Reeves (retired), Major General Frank R. McCoy, Admiral William H. Standley (retired), and Brigadier General Joseph T. McNarney of the Army Air Corps. The board publicly released its findings on January 23.

The Roberts Commission reported that none of the nation's political and military leaders were to blame for the attack. The commission did, however, fault Admiral Kimmel and Lieutenant General Short for a lack of readiness. The commanders, the board judged, neglected to confer regarding joint defense and failed to adopt adequate alert measures after receiving the war warnings from Washington. Although the report acknowledged that "there were deficiencies in personnel, weapons, equipment, and facilities to maintain all the defenses on a war footing for extended periods of time," those deficiencies, it noted, did not excuse the lack of preparation for attack.

Harshly, the commission concluded that Kimmel and Short were guilty of "a dereliction of duty." Each commander, it asserted, "failed properly to evaluate the seriousness of the situation. These errors of judgment were the effective causes for the success" of the surprise strike.

The verdict was humiliating for the two commanders, who until then had had spotless military careers. As Kimmel complained in a letter to Admiral Stark, "I do feel . . . that my crucifixion before the public has about reached the limit." Short later observed that "to be accused of dereliction of duty after almost forty years of loyal and competent service was beyond my comprehension." Some half-dozen investigations have since continued to probe the events and underlying issues of the Pearl Harbor attack.

Heading the inquiry

Associate U.S. Supreme Court Justice Owen J. Roberts headed President Roosevelt's special investigating team. Although the Roberts report praised "the high morale" of most military personnel during the emergency, it blamed Kimmel and Short for failing to respond adequately to warnings of a possible attack.

F2

Sea of fire

On Ford Island after the attack, officers in civilian suits approach a motor launch, attempting to get back to their ship, while oil fires blaze on the water by Battleship Row.

In the wake of the attack, Hawaii had been transformed into a high-security military post. Martial law was declared, and Hawaii's governor, Joseph B. Poindexter, turned over his authority to Short. The islands' new military government suspended many civil liberties. Citizens could be arrested and held without bail; private telephone conversations were monitored; curfews were set; and mail, newspapers, and radio broadcasts were censored.

Hawaii's Japanese, especially, now found themselves under suspicion. On the day of the attack, 370 Japanese Americans were rounded up, including local religious, business, and community leaders. First Lieutenant Cornelius C. Smith Jr. was one of many servicemen assigned to search the homes of local Japanese "with a fine-toothed comb" for contraband, including firearms, shortwave radio receivers, wireless transmitters, and cameras. In his diary entry, two days after the attack, he described Oahu's new atmosphere of fear: "Our Pacific Fleet was put out of commission by Jap carrier planes," he wrote. "Now here are these people, '100 percent loyal,' but are they? How powerful is the tie of blood? How strong that of adoption?" Fearful of arrest, many people of Japanese ancestry destroyed treasured family heirlooms—samurai swords, kimono sashes, even family pictures. Others prominently displayed signs of American patriotism, from U.S. flags to portraits of George Washington, Abraham Lincoln, and other presidents. Many even changed their family names, seeking to erase any links with Japanese culture or tradition.

Laid to rest

On December 8, at Kaneohe Bay Naval Air Station, crews bury the remains of many of those killed during the Pearl Harbor attack. The task of interring casualties went on for days. Every evening, recalled fireman Dan Wentreck, a bugler would sound taps. Then Wentreck and others would cover the hastily made pine coffins with earth, marking the mass graves with simple wooden stakes.

After Pearl Harbor, fear of Japanese sabotage spread quickly to the mainland. In February 1942, President Roosevelt signed Executive Order 9066, a measure that led to the evacuation of people of Japanese descent from the West Coast. Although some officials, including Secretary of the Navy Frank Knox, urged the forced removal of Hawaiian Japanese as well, Admiral Chester Nimitz successfully protested the measure. If Hawaii's 158,000 Japanese Americans—a third of the islands' population—were removed to mainland internment and relocation camps, he argued, thousands of loyal islanders would be incarcerated and much of Hawaii's economy, especially its agriculture, would be crippled. Although widespread evacuations were forestalled, 1,875 Hawaiians of Japanese ancestry were eventually confined to internment and relocation camps on the mainland.

Amid exaggerated rumors of enemy invasion, one member of the Japanese aerial strike force did, in fact, land alive and armed on

Hawaiian soil. At 2:00 P.M. on the day of the Pearl Harbor attack, Petty Officer First Class Shigenori Nishikaichi crash-landed his damaged plane on the remote island of Niihau at the western end of the Hawaiian chain. None of the Niihau islanders had heard of the attack, but one of them—Howard Kaleohano, who lived near the field where Nishikaichi landed—noticed bullet holes on the plane, which was painted with the emblems of the rising sun. Opening the pilot's canopy, Kaleohano disarmed Nishikaichi and confiscated his official papers.

For the next four days, local villagers kept the pilot under guard. Nishikaichi, however, managed to persuade one Japanese-American islander, Yoshito Harada, to obtain some guns and help him escape. Over the next two days, Nishikaichi and Harada threatened the villagers, demanding that they turn over Kaleohano and the pilot's papers. The two also searched Kaleohano's home for the documents; finding nothing, they set fire to the house on Saturday, December 13. Kaleohano, meanwhile, had left Niihau to obtain help, rowing for sixteen hours to the island of Kauai. Nishikaichi and Harada then captured two villagers, Ben Kanahele and his wife, Ella, and kept them hostage. Before Kaleohano could return with the authorities, Nishikaichi shot and seriously wounded Kanahele. Enraged, the villager then killed the pilot by hurling him

Detention of Japanese Americans

In 1941, 70 percent of the Japanese residing in the United States were American-born citizens. Beginning in March 1942, about 110,000 Japanese Americans on the West Coast were forced to leave their homes for wartime internment camps in remote regions of the country.

against a lava-rock wall and cutting his throat; Harada took his own life with a shotgun.

One other Japanese attacker found himself alone in Hawaii long after the Imperial strike force had departed. Ensign Kazuo Sakamaki, struggling to navigate his malfunctioning midget sub, had never successfully made it into Pearl Harbor. Instead, he and his crewman, Kiyoshi Inagaki, had stranded their vessel on a coral reef. On the morning after the attack, Lieutenant Phillip Willis was patroling with the Hawaiian National Guard when one of the men spotted the small, dark conning tower jutting from the surf. By that time, the two copilots had abandoned the sub, and Inagaki, weakened and exhausted, had drowned. Sakamaki, however, was still alive and had been carried by the breakers to the shore. Finally, Willis, recalled, Sakamaki "couldn't take it any longer" and came up to the beach. "His toes and fingers were shriveled up," Willis remembered. "He'd been in the water for hours. . . . He was clean shaven, hair clipped, ready for the final gesture for the emperor."

First prisoner of war

Soldiers captured Japanese midget submarine pilot Kazuo Sakamaki and took him prisoner after his vessel, *below,* was disabled on a coral reef. The morning of the attack, the Japanese strike force launched five midget submarines, each armed with two torpedoes, within ten miles of Pearl Harbor's entrance. After penetrating the harbor undetected and torpedoing ships during the attack, the subs were supposed to rendezvous with their mother ships, about seven miles west of the Hawaiian island of Lanai. The mother ships, however, never made contact with a single midget submarine after the attack, despite several searches. Sakamaki was the only midget-sub pilot who survived.

Sakamaki was America's first prisoner of war; he was the only member of the midget submarine force who survived the Pearl Harbor attack.

Japanese WWII winter flight suit

Three days later, Secretary of the Navy Frank Knox visited Pearl Harbor to see for himself the extent of and reasons for the damage. The human toll was heavy: 2,389 dead and 1,143 wounded. On the *Arizona* alone, 1,177 perished, out of a crew of 1,731, within the first ten minutes of the attack. Nearly 350 planes had been destroyed or damaged; twenty-one vessels had been crippled or sunk. Knox, in his report to Roosevelt, blamed Japanese agents in Hawaii, as well as insufficient defenses, for the success of the devastating strike. "The United States services were not on the alert," he concluded, "against the surprise air attack on Hawaii."

The two men most responsible for U.S. forces on Oahu, Admiral Husband Kimmel and Lieutenant General Walter Short, were held in part to blame. On December 16, the army relieved Short of his command, replacing him with Lieutenant General Delos C. Emmons, and Admiral Kimmel was relieved by Vice Admiral William S. Pye. On Christmas morning, Admiral Chester Nimitz replaced Pye, relieving him of his interim command of the Pacific Fleet.

JAPANESE-AMERICAN INTERNMENT

At War on the Home Front

The desert was bad enough. . . . The constant cyclonic storms loaded with sand and dust made it [worse]. After living in well-furnished homes with every modern convenience and suddenly forced to live the life of a dog is something which one cannot so readily forget."

—Joseph Yoshisuke Kurihara, Japanese American at Manzanar

On February 19, 1942, two months after the Pearl Harbor attack, President Roosevelt signed Executive Order 9066, which led to the forced removal of about 110,000 Japanese Americans from the West Coast to government internment camps. Anti-Japanese sentiment had been common on the U.S. mainland since the early 1900s, after thousands of Japanese immigrants arrived and settled on the Pacific Coast.

Once war erupted with Japan, rumors of Japanese espionage spread quickly. Lieutenant General John L. DeWitt, head of the army's Western Defense Command, began urging the U.S. War Department to remove every Japanese and Japanese American from the West Coast, declaring that "it makes no difference whether he is an American citizen or not." Despite misgivings, Secretary of War Stimson agreed, and Roosevelt issued his executive order.

At the end of March, tens of thousands of Japanese and Japanese Americans were forced to leave their homes and taken to hastily built assembly centers on fairgrounds and racetracks. Weeks later, they were transferred once again to ten bleak relocation camps in deserts and isolated areas of California, Arizona, Idaho, Utah, Colorado, Wyoming, and Arkansas. There, evacuees lived in crude barracks, fenced in by barbed wire and watched over by military police, until the camps were closed just a few months before the war's end.

In December 1944, the Supreme Court upheld the constitutionality of the forced evacuation; however, Justice Frank Murphy noted in dissent that the ruling went over "'the very brink of constitutional power' and falls into the ugly abyss of racism." Four years later, Congress gave $37 million in reparations to the internees—a fraction of the nearly $400 million in property losses that they suffered. In 1988, Congress officially acknowledged the injustice of the internment and awarded $20,000 to every individual who had been imprisoned. The reparations were sent with a signed apology from President Ronald Reagan.

Forced evacuation

With a few days' or weeks' notice, West Coast Japanese and Japanese Americans were ordered to pack what they could carry and leave their homes for bleak, isolated internment camps such as Manzanar, *below,* in the shadow of Mt. Whitney in the southern California desert. Imprisoned for nearly three years, many lost their homes, property, and businesses during the internment.

Salvage teams
Navy divers pose in front of a decompression chamber during salvage and recovery efforts in Pearl Harbor. On the *Nevada* alone, divers spent more than 950 hours under water in recovery operations.

Arriving in Pearl Harbor by flying boat, Nimitz passed the remains of five sunken battleships and boats loaded with the bodies of dead sailors. "It might have happened to me," he quietly told Kimmel when the two men shook hands later that day. Admiral Kimmel remained in Hawaii until January 1942, when the Roberts Commission—the first official investigation of the attack—completed its work. In February, he retired from the navy. Short retired from the army the next month.

In the harbor, salvage crews were moving quickly to recover and repair the fleet. The *Pennsylvania* had escaped serious damage; after initial repairs in the dry dock at Pearl Harbor, she sailed for Puget Sound on December 20, to be thoroughly modernized. By the same day the *Tennessee* had returned to service, and the *Maryland,* which had been flooded and bombed, was seaworthy and sailed for California's Mare Island Navy Yard. Repairs on the sunken *Nevada,* however, were far more difficult. On the day after the attack, the twisted metal, wreckage, and debris had been cleared away. Her decks and bulkheads were washed down, crews were already repainting, and her five-inch guns had been repaired. But it was not until February that the *Nevada* reached dry dock. Work on the ship "was a big job," civilian

Photo album from the Arizona

repair worker Ernest Pacheco, remembered, and it was a trying one; the smell of death, he recalled, clung to the inside of the vessel. The task of salvaging the ship was also dangerous. Two acetylene torch cutters were killed by hydrogen sulphide fumes. Others died below decks, following orders to salvage foul-weather gear. "We didn't know at the time that the chemicals in the raincoats and the boots, when mixed with salt water for a long time, made a gas," Pacheco recalled. Ten workers perished from the toxic fumes.

The *West Virginia,* blasted and sunk with nine torpedo hits, was not raised until May 1942. "You could have driven big trucks in her center. The destruction was unbelievable," recalled Shipfitter Third Class Louis Grabinski. Deep inside her hull, men had been trapped after the attack. For days after the raid, marine bugler Richard Fiske, standing guard, had heard tapping sounds coming from the hull, but rescuers had been unable to reach the sailors trapped inside. Months later, when the *West Virginia* was at last drained and dry, crews finally probed six decks down and opened her last watertight compartment. Fiske was one of the men who opened that last hatch. The light of their lantern revealed the bodies of three dead sailors. "The last marking on the calendar they had," Fiske recalled, "was December 24, 1941." The three had survived, trapped and alone, for seventeen days after the attack. The experience of finding the bodies was devastating; no one in the crew, Fiske said, was really the same again after that.

Fighting words

Immediately after the Japanese raid, the defiant American public rallied around a popular new slogan, "Remember Pearl Harbor." Only eight days after the attack, Don Reid and Sammy Kaye released their hit song by that name. An instant best-seller, the tune urged Americans to victory: "Let's remember Pearl Harbor as we go to meet the foe. Let's remember Pearl Harbor as we did the Alamo." Posters and signs appeared everywhere, uniting and inspiring the homefront to "Remember Pearl Harbor" and "Remember December 7th" as America mobilized for war.

For those who lived through it, the trauma of the attack "changed our complacent world completely," remembered Lieutenant Commander Ed Seiser. "Even the atmosphere, the sky, the sun, the ocean, our feeling of smugness. . . . Never before was so much concentrated hell heaped upon one place in so short a time." For Myrtle Watson, "what hurt and stuck" was the fact that so many young men died so defenselessly. Many of them, she recalled, "had gone to bed numb with Saturday night parties." Then suddenly, hobbling out of bed, "trying to get on their packs, pulling up zippers, and adjusting helmets," they awoke to a deadly reality "of bombs and bullets, signaling the end of something and the beginning of something else."

For everyone all over the United States, the attack on Pearl Harbor and its aftermath was a turning point. Shaken, grim, determined, Americans knew "there would be blood . . . there would be sweat," Henry Luce, editor of *Life* magazine, reflected; "so it has come to us." In the face of war, they rallied, despite bitter differences. "A new slogan is seen everywhere: 'Remember Pearl Harbor!'" Cornelius Smith wrote in his diary after the attack. "It has a ring about it like 'Remember the Alamo!' 'Remember the Maine!' I guess that years from now kids will see it in history books . . . but," he added, "that all belongs to another day."

SALVAGING DAMAGED SHIPS

Because Japanese bombers spared Pearl Harbor's dry dock and ship-repair facilities, salvage operations on the wrecked ships got underway immediately. First to be repaired were the most lightly damaged warships. Within weeks, the battleships Pennsylvania, Tennessee, *and* Maryland *had returned to service. Eventually, all but two of Pearl Harbor's eight battleships—the* Arizona *and the* Oklahoma*—were completely repaired, refitted, and returned to duty.*

One of the first priorities in the days after the attack was to salvage the ships' anti-aircraft guns and equipment. Divers recovered six fourteen-inch guns from the sunken wrecks of the *Arizona,* the *California,* and other disabled vessels. Meanwhile, salvage work proceeded quickly on the light cruiser *Helena.* After initial repairs at Pearl Harbor, she sailed for California's Mare Island Navy Yard in January 1942 to be refitted and modernized. The next month, work on the repair ship *Vestal* was completed at Pearl Harbor, and the light cruiser *Raleigh* left Hawaii for Mare Island for additional work. The destroyer *Shaw,* despite the cataclysmic explosion that tore the ship in two pieces, was also fitted with a new, temporary bow and sailed under its own steam for Mare Island in February.

USS Oklahoma

USS Nevada

USS Oklahoma

The *Oklahoma, far left column,* capsized by Japanese torpedoes, was righted on March 8, 1943, using a specially constructed system of shore-based electric winches. The battleship was too damaged to be returned to duty. Sold for scrap in December 1946, she sank five months later while being towed to the West Coast.

USS Nevada

The battleship *Nevada,* beached near Pearl Harbor's entrance and filled with water and oil, was patched, pumped dry, and towed into dry dock, *left,* on February 14, 1942.

On April 22, the *Nevada* sailed under her own power for Puget Sound Navy Yard for modernization. In June 1944, the battleship served in the Allied armada in the D-Day invasion of Normandy.

Work on the badly damaged battleships *Nevada* and *California* also began immediately. Crews made patches of steel and wood to plug the ships' bomb and torpedo holes, then pumped out the water before bringing the ships into dry dock. In April 1942, the *Nevada* left Pearl Harbor and sailed for Washington's Puget Sound Navy Yard for further work. The *California* left for Washington in October.

Even ships that had been considered a total loss were eventually repaired and returned to service. Although the hulls of the destroyers *Cassin* and *Downes* were too badly damaged to be saved, their fittings were shipped to Mare Island, where new hulls were assembled. The rebuilt *Downes* was recommissioned in November 1943, and the new *Cassin* rejoined the Pacific Fleet in February 1944. The mine-layer *Oglala*—capsized and shattered in the harbor—was also righted, refloated, repaired, and returned to duty in February 1944.

Three vessels, however, were beyond salvage. The capsized battleship *Oklahoma* was righted using twenty-one electric winches anchored on Ford Island. After she entered dry dock in December 1943, the badly damaged vessel's guns and machinery were removed, and the ship was decommissioned in September. The capsized target ship *Utah* was partly righted in 1944, but the navy abandoned further salvage attempts. The *Utah* and the fifty-eight men who lost their lives on board the ship remain undisturbed within the harbor. A USS *Utah* memorial was established on Ford Island in 1972. The *Arizona,* its front half demolished by catastrophic explosions, also remains where it sank on December 7, 1941, with the loss of 1,177 men.

Risky recovery work

Navy divers and salvage teams work in dangerous conditions in a gas-filled compartment of a damaged ship. Saltwater combined with man-made materials on the ships to create deadly hydrogen sulfide fumes, which claimed the lives of more than a dozen salvage workers.

In the days after the attack, tales of the Japanese navy's triumph—one of the greatest surprise strikes in naval history—spread quickly throughout Japan. "Soon everyone knew. 'Victory! Victory!' Things became raucous with the news," remembered navy officer Yoshida Toshio. Mighty America, the Japan Times *gloated, "trembles in her shoes." But the stunningly successful Pearl Harbor attack was just the opening move in a vast Japanese offensive, launched almost simultaneously across a five-thousand-mile front in the Pacific. Unleashed with the fury of a blitzkrieg, the onslaught was designed to neutralize American and British forces, leaving Japan free to seize its coveted prizes in Southeast Asia. American air power, concentrated at Pearl Harbor and Clark Field in the Philippines, was a central target. Within hours of the Hawaii attack, over a hundred Japanese fighters and bombers shrieked over the Philippine bases of America's Far East Air Corps, smashing eighteen of its thirty-five B-17 bombers on the ground and demolishing three-quarters of its fighter planes.*

THE LEGACY

Sweater from the USS Arizona

Japan was also moving to capture U.S. airstrips in the Pacific to position itself for land and sea invasions. Soon after the Pearl Harbor strike, Japanese planes hit America's island stronghold of Guam in the Marianas, as well as its Wake Island Pacific naval base. The same day, Japanese forces attacked Britain's weakly defended colonies in Asia, launching fierce aerial and land assaults on the Hong Kong territories and landing troops at Kota Bharu in Malaya, with the objective of reaching the capital of Singapore.

On December 10, Japan seized its first American possession. At dawn, a four-hundred man Japanese landing force came ashore at Guam, compelling the surrender of the U.S. garrison. Britain suffered a crushing naval defeat that same day. Off the coast of Malaya, eighty-eight Japanese torpedo planes and bombers, flying from Indochinese bases, swarmed over a British squadron of six warships, including the battleship *Prince of Wales* and the battle cruiser *Repulse.* With no carrier protection, both ships—the most powerful British vessels in Asia—sank to the bottom of the Gulf of Thailand, along with 840 men. "In my whole naval experience," Winston Churchill recollected, "I do not remember any naval blow so heavy or so painful." As the British Chief of the General Staff Sir Alan Brooke explained it, the sinking of the vessels meant "that from Africa eastward to America, through the Indian Ocean and the Pacific," Britain had now "lost control of the sea."

By Christmas Day, Japan had invaded the island of Borneo in the Dutch East Indies.

America at war

A youngster from New York City's Madison Square Boys' Club carries a bundle of papers trumpeting war news. Suddenly, after Pearl Harbor, Americans found themselves off the sidelines and actively at war, not only in Europe but across a vast theater of conflict in the Pacific.

JAPS DECLARE WAR
ATTACKED,
A SUNK
2¢
MIRROR
FINAL EDITION
INDIGESTION
Engineer Corps to
Red Ambassador Welcomed

America's defenders on Wake Island, after twelve days of aerial bombardment, had at last surrendered to Japan, and the British colony of Hong Kong—isolated and relentlessly attacked by land, air, and sea—finally capitulated. Japan had paralyzed American air and naval bases in the Pacific, knocked out Britain's naval power, and seized essential sources of petroleum less than one month after the opening of the war with the United States. Over the next six months, Japan's military offensive seemed unstoppable. In January, Manila, the capital of the Philippines, fell, and Japan expanded its gains in the Dutch East Indies. Japanese troops marched into Singapore, the strategic center of Britain's Asian colonies on February 8, 1942. Previously considered impregnable, with great guns facing the sea, Singapore was in fact defenseless from the rear, where the island bordered the Malayan jungle.

On February 15, after two hundred thousand Japanese troops invaded the capital from the mainland, Sir Arthur Percival turned the city over to Japan "under the shadow," Churchill said, "of a heavy and far-reaching defeat." Japanese soldiers then rapidly moved into Sumatra, placing Java—and the conquest of the Dutch East Indies—easily in reach. To try to stem the Japanese advance, the American, British, Australian, and Dutch allies combined their scattered forces but, far outmatched, lost most of their ships on February 27 in the Battle of the Java Sea. Japan, now unopposed, seized Java and compelled the Netherlands to surrender the

Losses in the Pacific

Within hours of the Pearl Harbor attack, Japanese planes bombed Wake Island, America's base in the north-central Pacific. On December 11, the American garrison drove off invasion forces, sinking two Japanese destroyers and damaging six other warships. On December 23, 1941, however, Japanese attackers captured Wake, renaming it Otori Shima (Bird Island) and taking 1,616 Americans prisoner. The conquest of Wake was part of a Japanese blitzkrieg through the Pacific and Southeast Asia in the months after Pearl Harbor. Right, U.S. Navy recruitment poster.

prized East Indies; it then quickly captured the Burmese capital of Rangoon.

Emperor Hirohito, receiving news of these stunning victories, was "beaming like a child," remembered Koichi Kido, Lord of the Privy Seal. "The fruits of war," the emperor observed, "are tumbling into our mouth almost too quickly." In fact, "victory disease" was growing rampant among Japan's military leaders. Admiral Isoroku Yamamoto, architect of the Pearl Harbor attack, warned against "this mindless rejoicing." Despite the fact that Japan had rapidly achieved its main objectives—expanding its empire and seizing raw materials while crushing Allied air and sea power—its military leaders were determined to continue the offensive. Now poised on the doorstep of Australia, Japan would "continue expanding from the areas we have already gained," a policy document declared, in order "to force Britain to submit and the United States to lose its will to fight."

For Americans, the first months of war after Pearl Harbor had been unquestionably grim. "We are losing," *Life* magazine conceded, "and . . . there is no evidence that the worldwide tide of battle has shifted in our favor." Still, although America was weakened by the devastation at Pearl Harbor, its capacity to rebuild had not diminished.

Japan's Conquests in the Pacific

The time has at last arrived when Nippon's aspiration and efforts to establish East Asia for East Asiatics, free from the Anglo-Saxon yoke, coincides exactly with the German-Italian aspiration to build a new order in Europe and to seek a future appropriate to their strength by liberating themselves from the Anglo-Saxon clutches."

—*Mainichi Shimbun* editorial, September 9, 1940

Beginning with its attack on American air and naval forces at Pearl Harbor, Japan launched a sweeping offensive across the Pacific and Southeast Asia. Within three months, Japanese forces had invaded Hong Kong, the Philippines, Guam, Thailand, Malaya, Singapore, British Borneo, and the Dutch East Indies.

Japan's plan was to expel the Western powers of the United States, Britain, and the Netherlands from Asia, then develop its newly conquered territories into the "Greater East Asian Co-prosperity Sphere." This international alliance would strengthen Japan's power and supply the vital resources it craved. Fortified by this expanded economic and strategic base, Japan's leaders believed that they would be able to win the war with China, where more than two million of their soldiers were entrenched, and

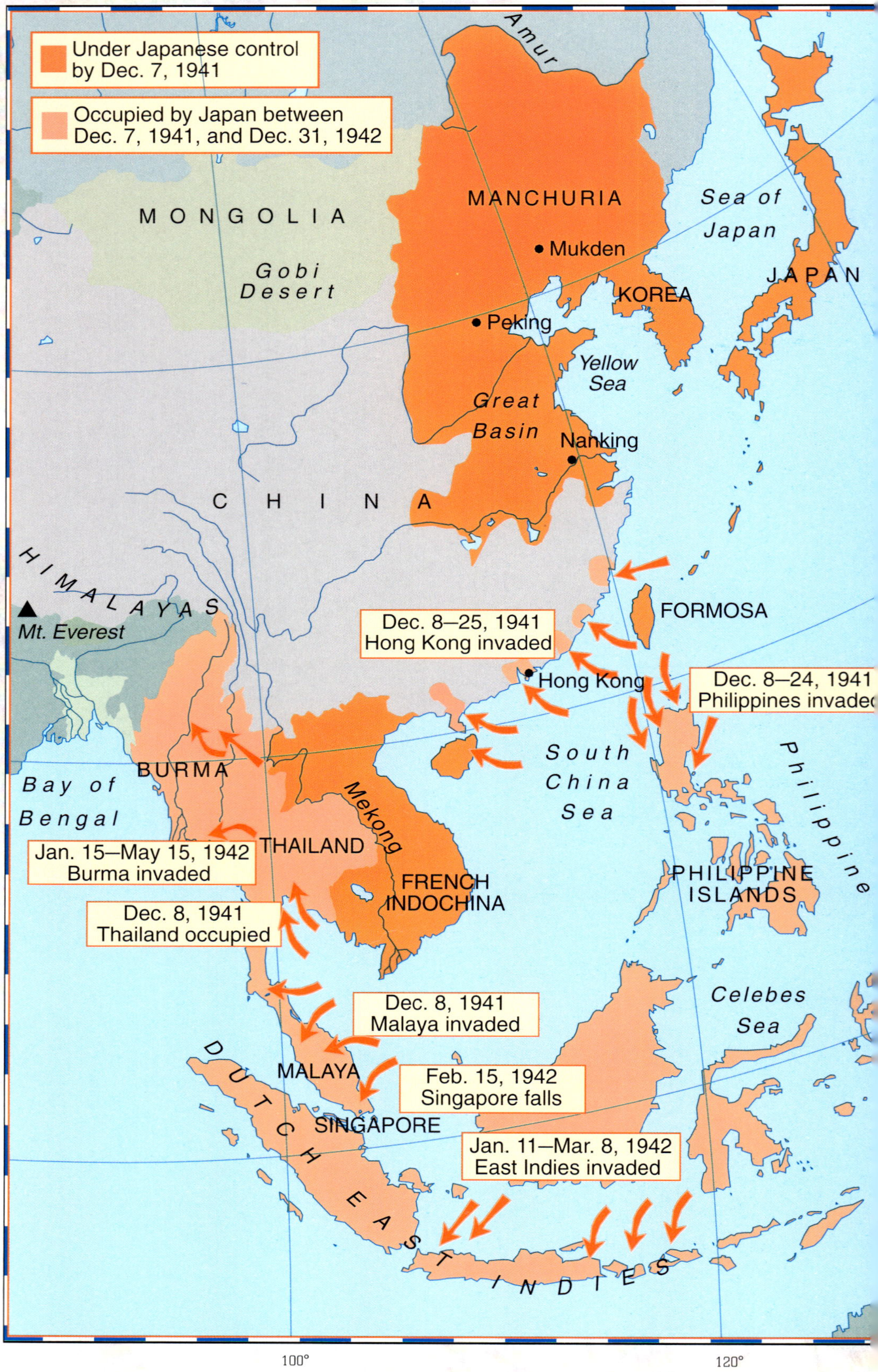

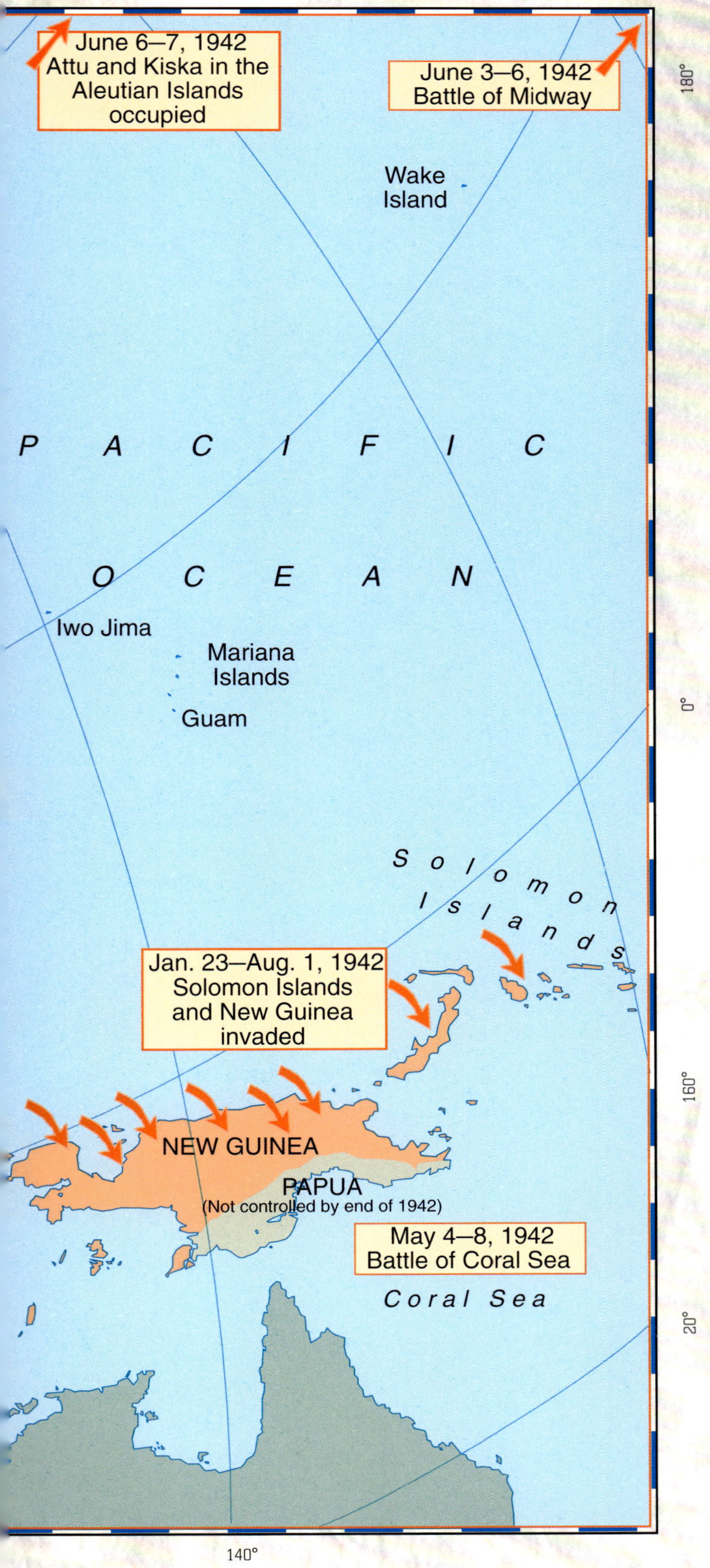

The Battle of Midway

From June 3 to 6, 1942, Japanese and American carrier forces clashed near Midway Island in the Pacific, *below*. American dive bombers sank four of the six Japanese carriers that had launched the surprise strike at Pearl Harbor. Japan also lost 250 aircraft and some ninety pilots in the battle. Midway was a turning point in the Pacific War; after the battle, Japan's once-unstoppable forces faced a mounting series of defeats.

eventually negotiate with the United States from a position of strength.

To shut off the flow of Allied troops and supplies into China, Japanese forces also advanced into Burma, conquering the country by the end of 1942. Japan simultaneously sought to strengthen its Pacific perimeter by seizing island bases in New Guinea, the Solomon Islands, and the Aleutians.

The cornerstone of Japan's Pacific strategy was to destroy the American carrier fleet at Midway Island, halfway between the United States and Japan in the Pacific. As Admiral Yamamoto's staff stated: "The success or failure of our entire strategy in the Pacific will be determined by . . . destroying the United States fleet, more particularly its carrier task forces. . . . By launching the proposed operations against Midway, we can succeed in drawing out the enemy's carrier strength and destroying it in decisive battle."

Midway proved to be decisive, but it turned the tide of war against Japan. On June 4 and 5, 1942, American dive bombers destroyed much of Japan's carrier striking force. With the core of its air and naval power crushed, Japan struggled unsuccessfully to maintain control of its expanded empire in the face of rapidly increasing Allied strength.

The attacking planes had spared essential targets. Pearl Harbor's machine shops and dry docks were only slightly damaged; as a result, all but three of the damaged warships were eventually salvaged or repaired. In addition, the harbor's fuel tanks, stored aboveground and filled to capacity on the day of the attack with 4.5 million barrels of oil, were untouched and able to continue supplying ships from the Pacific base. If the oil tanks had been hit, Admiral Kimmel reckoned, the Pacific Fleet would have been forced to withdraw to the West Coast, since no fuel was available anywhere else in the Pacific to keep it operating. Equally important was the fact that three aircraft carriers, out of the harbor on that Sunday morning, escaped destruction. Although the U.S. battleships had been damaged, the Pacific Fleet had not been utterly destroyed; and although Japan had dealt America a brutal blow, it had also unintentionally aroused its will to fight.

The Doolittle Raid

In April 1942, a B-25 bomber takes off from the deck of the *Hornet,* one of sixteen bound for a bombing mission over Tokyo, Yokohama, Kobe, and other urban centers in Japan. Led by Lieutenant Colonel James Doolittle, the raid boosted American morale and focused Japan's strategy on strengthening defenses in the Pacific.

After months of bad news from the Pacific, the U.S. Army air forces gave Japan its first taste of vulnerability. On the morning of April 18, 1942, sixteen B-25 bombers led by Lieutenant Colonel James Doolittle took off from the aircraft carrier *Hornet* and headed 550 miles west for Tokyo. Around noon, they reached their target and dropped bombs throughout the city, demolishing ninety buildings, killing fifty civilians, and destroying several tanks of precious fuel.

THE ARMY'S MOST DECORATED UNIT

Japanese-American Soldiers in Europe

Singled out for their courage in the European conflict were the U.S. Army's 100th Infantry Battalion and 442nd Regimental Combat Team, comprised of Americans of Japanese ancestry. Many of these Niseis—second-generation Japanese Americans—came from the islands of Hawaii, while others volunteered from internment camps on the U.S. mainland. After Pearl Harbor, many felt they had to prove their patriotism. As one Japanese American explained, "If you cut off my arm, it would bleed the same as a white man's would."

Anti-Japanese attitudes were common in the United States after the attack, but in June 1942 more than fourteen hundred Hawaiian Nisei army inductees transferred to the mainland for training, where they were formed into the 100th Infantry Battalion.

The 100th took part in fierce fighting in Italy from September 1943 to June 1944. Driving toward Rome, sustaining heavy casualties, the 100th was soon known as the army's "Purple Heart battalion." In June 1944, the 442nd Regimental Combat Team, made up of some twenty-six hundred Hawaiian Nisei volunteers and twelve hundred mainland Japanese Americans, arrived in Italy and absorbed the depleted force of the 100th. Troops of the combined 100th/442nd then began six months of intense fighting in France.

The Purple Heart

In October they staged the emergency rescue of three hundred men of the "Lost Battalion," a Texas unit that had been surrounded for a week in the mountains of northeastern France with little ammunition or food. The Nisei rescuers struggled for four days to reach the soldiers stranded behind enemy lines, battling machine guns and snipers for every yard of mountainous terrain. Finally, pinned down, they charged the machine guns, suffering huge losses, and broke through the lines to make the rescue.

By the end of the war, the 100th/442nd was known as the "Army's Most Dedicated Unit," with seven Presidential Distinguished Unit Citations. Many of the Nisei felt that "they had something extra to fight for, more than . . . average soldiers," explained First Lieutenant Masayuki Matsunaga. Since Pearl Harbor, he said, "They have their loyalty to prove." In the Pacific theater, Japanese Americans also played a vital role, serving as interpreters and intelligence agents in the army, navy, and marines.

Undaunted courage

Soldiers of the 442nd Regimental Combat Team fought with exceptional bravery in Italy and France. The unit, formed entirely of Japanese Americans, was created in April 1943, after ten thousand Hawaiian and twelve hundred mainland Nisei answered the army's call for fifteen hundred volunteers. In June, the 442nd absorbed the 100th Infantry Battalion, a unit of Hawaiian Nisei soldiers whose ranks had been decimated during brutal fighting in Italy. The combined 100th/442nd went on to earn seven Presidential Distinguished Unit Citations.

RUSSELL
ENOGAI
OKAIAVISI
VELLA LAVELLA
TREASURY
CHOISEUL
BOUGAINVILLE
CAPE GLOUCESTER
SAIDOR
NISSAN
EMIRAU
AITAPE
TUMLEO
BIAK

The* Ward *keeps score

Sailors and officers aboard the *Ward,* the ship that fired America's first shot against Japan on December 7, pose with their battle scoreboard in June 1944. Nearly all the men present were aboard the vessel when the Japanese attacked Pearl Harbor.

The bombers flew on to crash-land in China, but seventy-one of the eighty airmen eventually made it back to the United States. The bombing was scarcely noticed by the Japanese population but had a profound effect on the development of Japan's offensive strategy. Instead of widening their conquests in Southeast Asia and China, Japan's military leaders, viewing the Doolittle raid as an affront to the emperor, decided to safeguard Tokyo by expanding Japan's Pacific perimeter, targeting New Guinea and the southern Pacific Ocean.

Early in May, Japan mobilized for the capture of Port Moresby on New Guinea's southern coast. On May 7 and 8, two U.S. carriers—including the *Lexington,* which had escaped destruction at Pearl Harbor—intercepted the Japanese invasion fleet in the Battle of the Coral Sea. Although the *Lexington* was lost, the Japanese were forced to abandon their sea-based Port Moresby offensive. Yamamoto, his plans thwarted by U.S. carriers, was now determined to lure them into a final, decisively destructive naval showdown. Personally commanding a vast force of imperial warships, Yamamoto sailed for Midway Island—a base, he believed, that the Americans were certain to defend. His strike force included, under the command of Admiral Nagumo, four of the six aircraft carriers that had launched the surprise raid at Pearl Harbor—the *Akagi,* the *Kaga,* the *Soryu,* and the *Hiryu.*

Fateful decision

Vice Admiral Chuichi Nagumo, *right,* refused to order a third attack wave at Pearl Harbor to destroy remaining targets, including ship-repair and fuel-storage facilities. As a result, the United States was able to supply, maintain, and rebuild its Pacific Fleet.

Loss of the Lexington

The *Lexington, below,* was away from its home base at Pearl Harbor on December 7, but Japanese planes sank it in the Battle of the Coral Sea in May 1942.

America's Pacific Fleet was still weak, but six months after Pearl Harbor, U.S. intelligence uncovered Yamamoto's plan. Armed with that foreknowledge, Admiral Nimitz assembled a force made up of three aircraft carriers, eight cruisers, fifteen destroyers, and 120 land-based planes on Midway. Early on the morning of June 4, 1942, after preliminary engagements that favored the Japanese, American pilots turned the tide of battle. Appearing suddenly over the Japanese carriers, they dive-bombed the *Akagi,* the *Kaga,* and the *Soryu* as attack planes were refueling on their decks. Commander Mitsuo Fuchida, who led the air strike on Pearl Harbor, watched the American "Hell Divers" approach the *Akagi,* descending with a "terrifying scream." A bomb crashed into the carrier with a blinding flash. Deck plates reeled grotesquely, he recalled, and planes stood tail up belching livid flames. Gasoline and

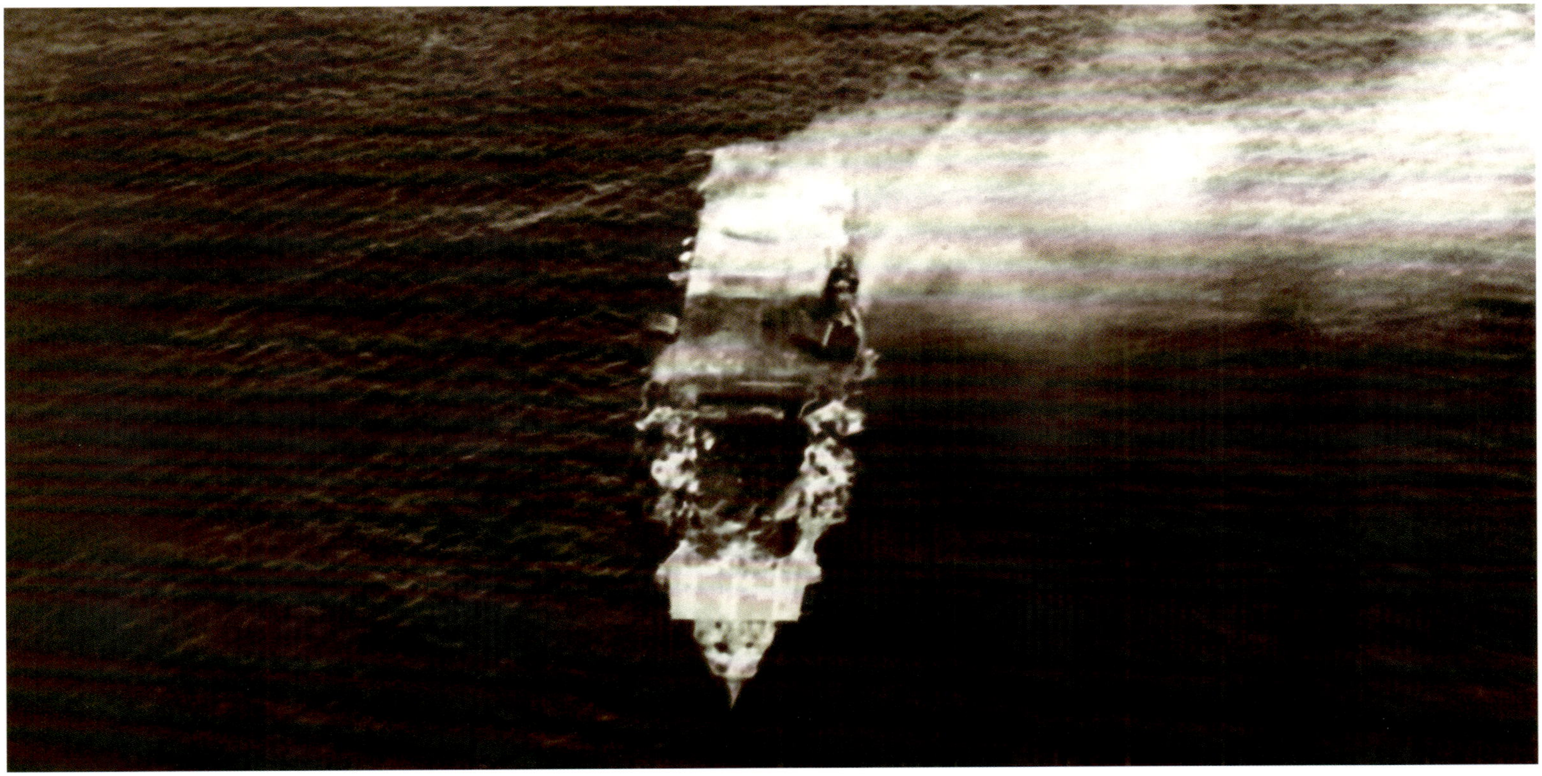

ammunition stores exploded, igniting fireballs and turning the carriers into infernos. After ten minutes of bombing, the *Akagi, Kaga,* and *Soryu* were flaming wrecks; the *Hiryu,* which escaped the first wave of dive bombers, was tracked down and crippled later that day. On June 6, Yamamoto ordered the remains of his once-powerful naval force to retreat. He had lost more than half his striking power in one battle, including most of the planes and carrier crews that had achieved his greatest triumph at Pearl Harbor. The scales of battle had tipped against the Japanese. From then on, they began losing as relentlessly as they had won during the first six months of war.

Losses at Midway

Nagumo's task force headed for Midway Island in June 1942, intending to wipe out the U.S. carrier fleet in a decisive naval battle. Instead, American dive bombers destroyed four Japanese carriers, including the *Hiryu, above,* turning the tide of war against Japan.

After Midway, the Allies went on the offensive. In August, U.S. marines came ashore on Guadalcanal Island in the Solomon chain, where Japan had been constructing an airstrip within striking distance of Australia. Japan abandoned the Solomons in February 1943, after six brutal months of air, land, and sea engagements. The next month, American and Australian bombers destroyed twelve Japanese ships off New Guinea, and in April, Admiral Yamamoto was shot down and killed in a U.S. air ambush above the Solomons.

An audio recording made for a GI

Fall of the Axis Powers

Ending the War in Europe

In the summer of 1940, Hitler had been determined to "crush Britain," invading it after devastating air attacks. After his Luftwaffe *had been repulsed by the Royal Air Force, however, the Führer postponed plans for invading Britain and looked to expand Nazi influence south and east instead.*

Mobilizing in the Mediterranean, German troops rapidly seized Greece, Libya, and Yugoslavia. At the same time, Hitler began laying plans for a massive invasion of Russia. "German victory is incompatible with Russian ideology," he informed his military commanders. "Russia must be smashed as soon as possible." Hitler believed his eastern invasion would be swiftly executed. On June 22, 1941, in a surprise attack, more than three million German soldiers and thirty-five hundred armored vehicles crossed the Soviet border, crushing Stalin's armies of resistance as they drove northward, east, and south. Only two weeks after the invasion, Hitler's army chief of staff believed the Germans had already won, but instead, as Nazi forces approached Moscow in October, they faced the onslaught of the Russian winter. Ill-clothed and ill-equipped for winter battle, and with supplies strained over enormous distances, Hitler's eastern offensive stalled.

Allied victories

In Tunisia, *left,* Allied troops expel Axis prisoners of war from conquered territory in July 1943, following the successful British and American invasion of North Africa.

Ruins of war

U.S. Private Paul Oglesby stands reverently before the bomb-damaged altar of a church in Acerno, Italy, *below.*

At the same time, the Soviets were mobilizing new sources of strength. Worried that Japan, an Axis ally, was planning to invade the Soviet Union from Manchuria, Stalin had massed troops along the Siberian border. When Japan chose to attack south instead, Soviet leaders transferred those seasoned forces to the German front. On December 6, 1941, the day before the Pearl Harbor strike, Soviet troops launched an effective counterattack that demoralized the hungry and exhausted Germans, pinning them down for months in the Russian cold.

Throughout the next year, while the campaign on the Eastern Front strained German manpower and resources, Nazi forces continued to wage war on other fronts. German troops in North Africa launched a summer offensive against Egypt, but they were defeated in late October by the British. Within days, a joint British and American armada landed in North Africa, the first U.S. initiative in the European war. By May 13, 1943, the Allies had driven the German and Italian armies from North Africa. The Americans and British launched an invasion of Sicily two months later, and on July 25, Mussolini fell. In September the Allies invaded Italy, and for the next eighteen months they fiercely battled the Germans for control of the peninsula.

By the end of 1943, the Soviets were pushing back Hitler's armies on the Eastern Front, and the Axis Powers had lost their grip on North Africa. Although German U-boats had long disrupted Allied supply lines in the Atlantic, that strategy was now thwarted by improved Allied patrols. After meeting in Tehran in late November, Roosevelt, Churchill, and Stalin expressed their confidence that momentum was now shifting against Hitler. "No power on earth," they stated in a communiqué, "can prevent our destroying the German armies by land, their U-boats by sea, and their warplanes from the air. Our attacks will be relentless and increasing."

On June 4, 1944, Allied forces captured Rome, and two days later they launched a cross-channel invasion of western Europe. An armada of more than two thousand ships, four thousand landing craft, and ten thousand planes—the greatest amphibious force ever assembled—converged on the beaches of Normandy, landing 156,000 American, British, and Canadian troops in northern France. By the end of the next month, nearly two million Allied troops were fighting their way south across occupied French territory. The Allies liberated Paris from the Germans on August 25. From there, they pushed through eastern France toward the Rhine River. The end was now in sight, an Allied intelligence report predicted: "The strength of the German armies in the west has been shattered. Paris belongs to France again, and the Allied armies are streaming toward the frontiers of the Reich."

German resistance, however, remained powerful along the Rhine. Although Allied bombing raids led to severe shortages of fuel, synthetic rubber, and medical supplies in Germany, Nazi forces kept the Allies locked in a winter war of attrition west of the German border.

Finally, in late March, Allied forces crossed the Rhine. Meanwhile, from the east, Stalin's armies had expelled the Nazis from their country and driven them westward across Poland, Czechoslovakia, Hungary, and Romania. The Soviets now occupied Germany's eastern sector, and the Allies were approaching from the west. With Berlin encircled, Hitler, isolated in his bunker, committed suicide on April 30. On May 8, 1945, German forces surrendered. The war in Europe was now over, but the war in the Pacific raged on.

D-Day invasion

U.S. troops, *left,* struggle through water and German gunfire to reach the beaches of Normandy on D-Day, June 6, 1944.

Victory in Europe

In London's Piccadilly Circus, civilians and U.S. servicemen, *below,* celebrate Germany's surrender in May 1945. "This is a solemn but glorious hour," British Prime Minister Winston Churchill declared.

The United States was reaping the fruits of its naval expansion, as powerful new aircraft carriers, warships, and submarines swelled the fleet. By the end of 1943, Japan was losing its grip over the edges of its overextended empire, and strengthened Allied forces continued the offensive, recapturing territory in Southeast Asia and expelling Japan, island by island, from its Pacific strongholds.

Over the course of the next year, the Allies captured the Marianas, New Guinea, the Solomons, the Marshalls, and other Japanese Pacific bases.

They annihilated Japan's carrier strength, and in October 1944, American forces landed in the Philippines. In February 1945, with U.S. troops now in Manila, American marines captured the ferociously defended island of Iwo Jima, less than 800 miles east of Japan. On April 1, American forces took Okinawa, only 350 miles from the Japanese coast. Now began the devastating endgame of the war. With its planes within striking distance of Japan, the United States sent waves of B-29s on catastrophic firebombing raids on Tokyo and other urban centers, including Nagayo, Kobe, and Osaka, killing more than a hundred thousand Japanese citizens and obliterating huge industrial and residential sections of the cities.

Planning the peace

British Prime Minister Churchill, U.S. President Truman, and Soviet Premier Josef Stalin, *left,* open the Potsdam Conference, held outside Berlin from July 17 to August 2, 1945. The leaders of the "Big Three" Allied powers negotiated issues such as the occupation and administration of Germany and the new postwar boundaries of Poland.

Hirohito's broadcast

At noon on August 15, 1945, workers at a company in Osaka, Japan, *right,* listen to a radio announcement by Emperor Hirohito, declaring Japan's unconditional surrender to the Allies. It was the first time that most Japanese citizens had heard their emperor's voice. Nine days earlier, the United States had detonated an atomic bomb over the Japanese city of Hiroshima, *far right,* instantly killing some eighty thousand people.

At the same time, the Americans were developing a fearsome new explosive weapon, the atomic bomb. On April 12, 1945—the day that President Franklin Roosevelt died of a cerebral hemorrhage—Secretary of War Henry L. Stimson told the new president, Harry S Truman, that the country was developing an unimaginably powerful new weapon. The A-bomb was successfully detonated at a test site near Alamogordo, New Mexico, three months later, on July 16, 1945. The next day, Truman was beginning meetings with Churchill and Stalin at Potsdam, outside Berlin, to discuss peace terms following the Allied victory in Europe. Stimson, receiving news about the test, informed President Truman that the results had been successful beyond anyone's "most optimistic expectations." On July 26, the Allies issued the Potsdam Declaration to Japan. The ultimatum demanded the "unconditional surrender" of Japan's armed forces; if the Imperial government did not comply, it warned, the alternative would be "prompt and utter destruction."

Japan's leaders refused to meet the Allies' demands. Eight days later, on August 6, 1945, an American B-29 bomber dropped an atomic bomb over the Japanese city of Hiroshima; in a blinding flash, some eighty thousand people lost their lives. On August 9, a second atomic bomb devastated the southern Japanese city of Nagasaki. The following day, Emperor Hirohito at last made the "sacred decision" to surrender, and on August 15, the people of Japan heard their Emperor's high-pitched, stilted voice for the first time. "The war situation," Hirohito told them in a taped radio broadcast, "has developed not necessarily to Japan's advantage. . . . Should we continue to fight, it would . . . result in an ultimate collapse and obliteration of the Japanese nation. . . . We have resolved to pave the way for a grand peace for all the generations to come by enduring the unendurable and suffering what is unsufferable."

The end of war

Sailors, officers, and dignitaries crowd the battleship *Missouri, above,* on the morning of September 2, 1945, during Japan's formal surrender to the Allies. At right, Mamoru Shigemitsu *(left, with cane)* and General Yoshijuro Umezu *(front row, right)* prepare to sign the official papers for Japan.

Japan's official surrender came on September 2. A vast number of Allied warships filled Tokyo Bay for the historic ceremony—among them was the *West Virginia,* a battleship that, nearly four years earlier, had been blasted and sunk in Pearl Harbor by Japanese torpedoes and bombs.

News of defeat

On the island of Guam, Japanese prisoners of war listen to Emperor Hirohito's broadcast announcing Japan's surrender.

As Mamoru Shigemitsu, Japan's foreign minister, stiffly climbed aboard the *Missouri* to sign the formal surrender documents, above him on the battleship fluttered the same American flag that had flown over the U.S. Capitol on December 7, 1941. The atmosphere on board ship was tense; the *Missouri,* recalled Shigemitsu's secretary, Toshikazu Kase, was "packed to suffocation" with "representatives, journalists, spectators, an assembly of brass, braid and brand"—Americans, British, Australians, Chinese, Soviets, and French. General Douglas MacArthur, presiding over the brief proceedings, declared his hope that "a better world shall emerge out of the blood and carnage of the past." Kase "tried to preserve with utmost sangfroid the dignity of defeat," he recollected, "but it was difficult." After all of the surrender documents were signed, MacArthur closed the ceremony; a dramatic flight of nearly two thousand American planes then thundered above the crowded bay, powerfully signaling the end of the Pacific War.

Sailor's scrapbook

The war was over—but Japan's first devastating blow was not forgotten. Since the Roberts Commission had first released its findings in 1942, other investigations of the Pearl Harbor attack had attempted to understand why the United States had been caught so unprepared and who should be held responsible. In 1944, Congress authorized an Army-Navy Court of Inquiry to conduct a second probe into the reasons for the disaster. The navy's report focused on the lack of communication from Washington; exonerating Admiral Kimmel, it noted that Admiral Stark had not provided him with all the advance knowledge available. The army board also faulted General George Marshall and the War Department for failing to keep Lieutenant General Short adequately informed. Following the release of the army and navy reports after the war, a third inquiry—a joint Congressional Committee Investigation—was authorized in 1945. Its findings, contained in a thirty-nine-volume study of the attack, differed from the Army-Navy Court by faulting Kimmel and Short for their decisions. Although the congressional inquiry did not claim that the commanders had been derelict in their duties, it did criticize them for lack of readiness. At the same time, the joint committee acknowledged the role that poor communication had played in relations among the Administration, the armed forces, and the various branches of the military.

In 1995, fifty-four years after the attack, the Defense Department convened yet another investigation—this time to judge whether the treatment of Admiral

Signing the peace

Surrounded by representatives of the Allied forces, General Douglas MacArthur signs Japan's surrender document aboard the USS *Missouri* on September 2, 1945. To mark the end of the Pacific War, Allied aircraft carriers, battleships, cruisers, destroyers, and landing vessels filled Tokyo Bay beneath Mount Fuji. Among the warships was the battleship *West Virginia.* Severely damaged by the Japanese at Pearl Harbor, the *West Virginia* had been salvaged and modernized, then served in the Pacific during the last year of the war.

Kimmel and Lieutenant General Short had been excessively harsh. The report, by Under Secretary of Defense Edwin Dorn, concluded that responsibility for the Pearl Harbor disaster "should be broadly shared." Resources were scarce, and information-sharing and coordination were inadequate. "The run-up to Pearl Harbor," the report noted, "was fraught with miscommunication, oversights, and lack of follow-up." The Japanese attack itself was brilliantly conceived, and the Hawaii commanders had also made errors of judgment. Both men, the study concluded, "suffered greatly for Pearl Harbor. They lost men for whom they are responsible. They felt that too much of the blame was placed on them"; as commanders, however, the report held them accountable. Admiral Kimmel, who was relieved of command in mid-December 1941, struggled for the rest of his life to restore his reputation; he died in 1968 at the age of eighty-six. Lieutenant General Short left the army in 1942 and died seven years later.

USS Arizona _Memorial_

Since 1980, the National Park Service has administered the USS *Arizona* Memorial, honoring those who died on the morning of the Pearl Harbor attack.

As debate about the attack continued to rage after the war, plans were also set in motion to build an official memorial to Pearl Harbor. The Territory (soon to be state) of Hawaii acted first, naming a Pacific

War Memorial Commission in 1949. It was another ten years, however, before the navy moved ahead with plans for a Pearl Harbor memorial at the site. Designed by Alfred Preis, the USS *Arizona* Memorial—dedicated on Memorial Day of 1962 to all who perished on the morning of December 7, 1941—was built in the form of an enclosed bridge above the sunken battleship. Inside the building are inscribed the names of the 1,177 men who died on the *Arizona* in the first violent minutes of the attack.

Beneath the bridge, the *Arizona* is still visible under the water, mottled green and golden with corrosion and colonies of aquatic life. Since 1983, National Park Service divers, often assisted by the U.S. Navy, have explored and mapped the *Arizona* and the *Utah,* the two ships that still rest on the harbor bottom, taking care never to disturb areas where bodies of the crew members remain. Amid the *Arizona*'s debris lie photographs that have been tossed into the water by family members of the deceased—"mementos from the living to the dead," observed diver Daniel Lenihan. These images, of siblings, children, and grandchildren, may be a way for those living to share with the men who still lie on the *Arizona* the joys and sorrows of offspring they have never known. Nearby on the sunken battleship, in the well of Turrett No. IV, are funeral urns, placed by National Park Service divers, of *Arizona* crew members who died more recently and wished to be laid to rest beside the bodies of their long-dead shipmates.

"Remember Pearl Harbor" patch

A day to remember

In 1942 sailors in Hawaiian tradition drape leis over the grave markers of those killed on December 7, 1941. Americans have never forgotten the shock and the losses of Pearl Harbor. In 1942, President Roosevelt designated December 7 as Pearl Harbor Day, "a day of silence in remembrance of the great infamy." Each year, more than 1.5 million people make a pilgrimage to Pearl Harbor and the USS *Arizona* Memorial. Older visitors, according to National Park Service historian Daniel Martinez, "see Pearl Harbor as a touchstone, and they come here to fulfill a patriotic duty. Young people think it's a tourist attraction," but then, he added, "the reality of what this place means hits them between the eyes."

For many who survived December 7, 1941, the shock and recollections never faded. Musician First Class Warren G. Harding maintained his own personal ritual of remembrance. The day after the attack, Harding discovered his trombone—safe but dented—inside the hulk of the shattered *California*. He never played it again, but for decades after the war, while he was busy selling real estate in Florida, he kept it in his bedroom on a stand and polished it faithfully every December 7. For Private Leslie Le Fan, memories came frequently, sometimes stirred by the subtle scent of pinewood on a breeze. After the Japanese attack, Le Fan had stood watch over the rough-hewn coffins of young men who had perished in the airfields and Pearl Harbor that Sunday morning. As crews covered the fresh graves with earth, "there were grown sailors and marines," he recalled, "big men, who were crying. . . . They had lost buddies; they had lost friends; they had lost their ships; they had lost everything. . . ." Years later, working in the circulation department of a newspaper in Temple, Texas, Le Fan said he could still smell fresh pinewood, and the memory would carry him back to Oahu Cemetery, where he saw blood and oil seeping out of the rough pine boxes and knew that, only yesterday, all those young men had been alive.

***Return of the* California**

The *California* sails full-speed toward Pearl Harbor in May 1944, after being repaired and modernized at Puget Sound Navy Yard. Fitted with a new superstructure, the battleship is returning to duty in the Pacific. *Painting by C. S. Bailey.*

Bailey

REMEMBERING PEARL HARBOR

To those who witnessed it, the attack on Pearl Harbor was a turning point—two hours that irrevocably changed the course of life and history. For the nation that day, the war began, triggering massive shifts in political and social forces, accelerating scientific research, and redefining America's role on the global stage. To the men and women who survived it, too, Pearl Harbor was a border between one world and another, a frontier that some never entirely left behind.

Paradise lost

Gordon Jones remembers how sweet Pearl Harbor's air smelled—"like blossoms"—when he first stepped off the ship from San Diego on December 1, 1941. The eighteen-year-old New Jersey native and his older brother, Earl, went straight to Kaneohe Bay Naval Air Station on Oahu's eastern shore, where they started duty as naval aviation mechanics. To the brothers, the base seemed close to paradise after the gritty poverty and unemployment they had grown up with on the mainland. Kaneohe Bay was brand new, and the chow was great. "Man, we could even go back for seconds," Jones recalled.

Out of the flames

Gordon Jones, *left*, was at Kaneohe Bay Naval Air Station when the Japanese attacked. Between the first and second waves, Jones, *above* (bending over plane), helped drag burning PBY flying boats onto the beach. Today, with the Pearl Harbor Survivors Association, he speaks to high-school students about the importance of being prepared.

He had gotten up early on Sunday, December 7, planning to go sightseeing with a friend, when he suddenly heard bursts of machine gun fire, then saw smoke billowing from hangars and planes swarming low over the base, spraying bullets wildly through their propellers. "We saw the red rising-sun 'meatballs' on the wings," Jones remembered, "but we hardly knew who the Japanese were or how they could even get here."

Earl was hit during the raid. A piece of shrapnel from a bomb lodged in his hip. Nearly sixty years later, he still suffers from the deep, disabling wound. Gordon has his own physical reminders: a piece of shrapnel that he found from another bomb at Kaneohe Bay and a handful of bullets from a

Japanese fighter plane. Regularly, he visits classrooms of high-school students and passes these grim souvenirs around. "We were so young and unprepared," he explains. "I want kids to know about Pearl Harbor and to realize that the unthinkable could happen again."

Wings of forgiveness

The leader of Japan's aerial attack on December 7, 1941, was Mitsuo Fuchida, an imperial navy pilot whose heart, he said, was filled with revenge as he flew over Pearl Harbor. In June 1942, Fuchida was present at the Battle of Midway, where he was severely wounded. The flier chronicled his experiences, after the war, in several books, including *The Truth of the Pearl Harbor Operation* and *Midway: The Battle That Doomed Japan.* Then, in 1949, he converted to Christianity after watching American missionaries feeding the starving in Tokyo. Fuchida hoped, he said, "to help young people of Japan learn a great love for America" through his faith. He, too, became a missionary, promoting peace, revisiting Pearl Harbor, and traveling widely in the United States. Fuchida retired in Japan and died there in May 1976.

New mission

After the war, Commander Mitsuo Fuchida, *below,* leader of Japan's aerial strike force, began a new life on the land, raising chickens and crops on a small farm in Nara, Japan. He converted to Christianity and, in 1952, traveled across the United States with the Worldwide Christian Missionary Army of Sky Pilots.

War games

The day the bombs fell on Oahu, eight-year-old John Bowles stood outside in Honolulu and stared at the sky, watching American and Japanese planes blasting each other in a dogfight overhead. "I had a feeling of awe that day," he remembered, that life could change so drastically—and dangerously—so fast.

The attack by Japan had special meaning for his family. Bowles was born near Tokyo, where his grandparents were missionaries and his father had a practice as a doctor. In 1936, as military leaders rose to power in Japan, Bowles's immediate family decided to leave Tokyo and move to Honolulu. On December 7, 1941 (his older sister's twelfth birthday), Bowles was riding to Sunday school in his father's car when he saw what he thought was a "sham battle"—planes flashing overhead and smoke rising from the warships in Pearl Harbor. As soon as he reached church, he heard the news.

For Bowles, the world changed suddenly, filled with exciting, often frightening, events. In the weeks after the attack, he and his sister would hitch rides in army convoys, watch troops practice landings on the beach, and invite lonely soldiers home for dinner. He still remembers the flare parachutes and plane-spotter guides the soldiers gave him as presents. He also remembers the curfews and blackouts as well as the miles of barbed wire and machine-gun nests near his family's beach house. And Bowles never forgot the pain suffered by local Japanese families. Officials arrested husbands and fathers, and many who remained at home were shunned by people they had long considered friends.

"The tragedy and disruption of war was very evident to me," Bowles said. "I've never been able to erase it from my mind." There are certainly lessons to be gleaned from the ordeal, he reflected, "but I'm not sure they are ones we've ever learned."

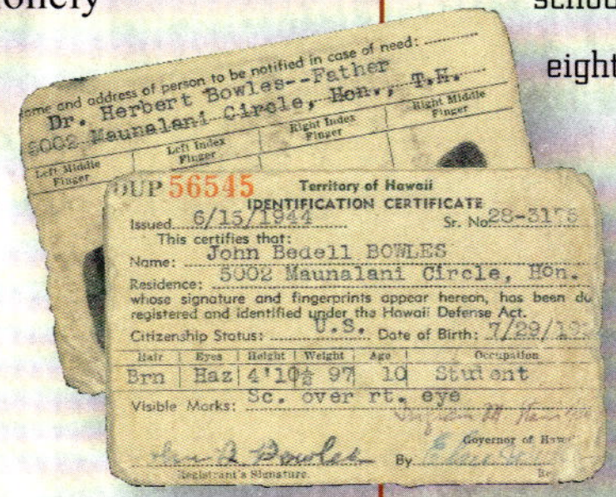

School security

In the days after the Japanese raid, Honolulu school children like eight-year-old John Bowles, *below,* were fingerprinted and issued gas masks and identification cards, *left.* Bowles' family had a beach house on Oahu's north shore. Bowles remembers, in the weeks of attack, getting a lift to the local store in an army tank and playing volleyball with soldiers who were manning machine-gun nests along the beach.

Shunned by history

For most of 1941, Takeo Yoshikawa served as Japan's eyes on the island of Oahu, gathering information that was crucial to the Pearl Harbor attack. While posing as a low-level functionary in the Honolulu consulate, he spied on Pearl Harbor and other bases, passing key details to the operation's planners in Tokyo. After the attack, Yoshikawa was interned in Arizona before being sent back to Japan in an exchange of diplomats. When Americans occupied his country after the war, Yoshikawa hid in a monastery, fearful that he would be executed for spying. He was never rewarded by Japan; military officials denied his request for a pension, insisting that no Japanese agent ever spied on Pearl Harbor before the surprise attack. Many Japanese, he reflected, blamed him for helping to start a war that ended terribly with the atomic bomb; they turned their backs, he said, on "a spy whose country had lost the war."

The last dance

The sounds of battle coming out of Pearl Harbor's Bloch Arena on the night of Saturday, December 6, 1941, were swinging hits and big-band, brassy numbers, played by navy bands fighting for the trophy in the Pacific Fleet's "Battle of Music." Tapping her feet, sitting on the floor close by the band, was a ten-year-old music lover named Pat Thompson (then Pat Campbell), who was living with her parents in navy housing. Thompson already had a reputation for her dancing, and when it was time to play the jitterbug, the band's announcer asked if anybody wanted to take a turn around the dance floor with the girl. A seventeen-year-old sailor bounded out of the bleachers, and he and Thompson danced off to capture the navy's 1941 jitterbug championship trophy that night. "I will never forget that evening," Thompson recalled—or the next morning, Sunday, December 7, when she heard the drone of Japanese planes over her house and saw the bombs blasting the ships inside the harbor.

She never saw her jitterbug partner again. Nearly sixty years later, she still wondered what had happened to him, whether he lost his life that Sunday morning or had survived the surprise attack and perhaps the war. It was, she said, her "one piece of unfinished business." In May 2000, Thompson, formerly a longtime administrative assistant for the San Diego Chargers football team, placed an article in the *Pearl Harbor Gram,* a newsletter for survivors of the disaster, hoping that a reader might remember the "Battle of Music" and perhaps know what became of the young sailor she danced with. Within two months, Thompson had a phone call from the missing seaman, Jack Evans, now a retired navy captain who, it turned out, lived just fifteen miles away.

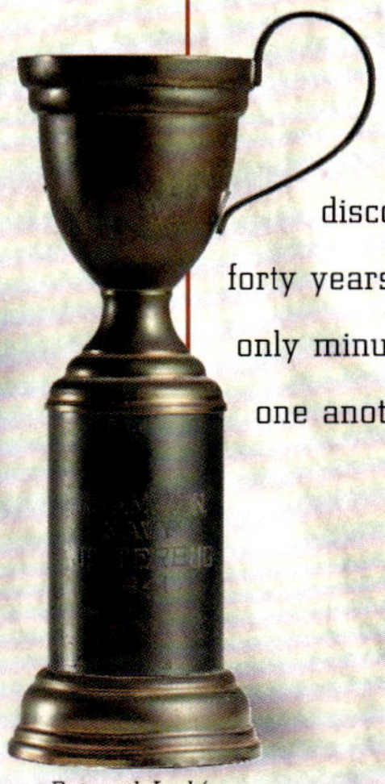

Pat and Jack's jitterbug trophy

The morning after their championship dance, Evans was on board the *Tennessee,* polishing his shoes for church, when Japanese planes shrieked over the harbor. Climbing to his battle station in the foretop, 110 feet above the water, he watched the *Oklahoma* roll over and explosions wrack the *Arizona,* dodging chunks of metal blasted from the ship high in the air. Wounded in the leg by a piece of shrapnel, he was too frightened to notice that he was bleeding. Hours later, he was still at his station, watching small boats dragging the bodies of dead men to the shore.

When he learned of Thompson's article, Evans started to weep, remembering those hours before the world changed forever at Pearl Harbor. He and the "swinging ten-year-old" he had danced with reconnected—with each other and with that last, footloose night before the war.

Stepping back in time

The night before the Japanese attack, seventeen-year-old Jack Evans, *below left,* won the 1941 navy jitterbug trophy with talented ten-year-old dance lover Pat Campbell, *below right.* The next day, Jack was looking forward to eating a home-cooked dinner with Pat's family, but instead, he ended up in his battle station on the *Tennessee,* dodging bullets, bombs, and shrapnel during the raid. They lost touch, but fifty-nine years later, the jitterbuggers, *right,* met again. Jack and his championship dance partner, now Pat Campbell Thompson, discovered that for forty years they have lived only minutes away from one another in California.

Selected Bibliography

Allen, Thomas B. "Pearl Harbor: A Return to the Day of Infamy." *National Geographic,* December 1991.

Army Times editors. *Pearl Harbor and Hawaii: A Military History.* New York: Bonanza Books, 1971.

Bix, Herbert P. *Hirohito and the Making of Modern Japan.* New York: HarperCollins Publishers, 2000.

Butterfield, Roger. *FDR.* New York: Harper & Row, 1963.

Borg, Dorothy, and Shumpei Okamoto, eds. *Pearl Harbor as History: Japanese-American Relations, 1931–41.* New York: Columbia University Press, 1973.

Burns, James MacGregor. *Roosevelt: The Soldier of Freedom.* New York: Harcourt Brace Jovanovich, 1970.

Clark, Blake. *Remember Pearl Harbor.* New York: Harper & Brothers, 1942.

Conroy, Hilary, and Harry Wray, eds. *Pearl Harbor Reexamined: Prologue to the Pacific War.* Honolulu: University of Hawaii Press, 1990.

Cook, Haruko Taya, and Theodore F. Cook. *Japan at War: An Oral History.* New York: The New Press, 1992.

Deac, Will. "The Pearl Harbor Spy Provided Valuable Intelligence to Japanese War Planners Prior to the Surprise Attack." *World War II,* May 1997.

Garrett, Betty. "A Date with a Bombing." *American Heritage,* December 1991.

Goldstein, Donald M., and Katherine V. Dillon, eds. *The Pearl Harbor Papers.* Washington, D.C.: Brassey's, 1993.

Heinrichs, Waldo. *Threshold of War.* Oxford: Oxford University Press, 1988.

Hoyt, Edwin P. *Japan's War.* New York: Da Capo Press, 1986.

Iriye, Akira. *The Origins of the Second World War in Asia and the Pacific.* London: Longman, 1987.

———, *Pearl Harbor and the Coming of the Pacific War.* Boston: Bedford/St. Martin's, 1999.

Keegan, John. *The Times Atlas of the Second World War.* London: Times Books, 1989.

———, *The Second World War.* New York: Viking Penguin, 1990.

Kennedy, David M. *Freedom from Fear: The American People in Depression and War, 1929–1945.* New York: Oxford University Press, 1999.

La Forte, Robert S., and Ronald E. Marcello. *Remembering Pearl Harbor.* Wilmington, Delaware: SR Books, 1991.

Landauer, Lyndall, and Donald Landauer. *Pearl: The History of the United States Navy in Pearl Harbor.* South Lake Tahoe, California: Flying Cloud Press, 1999.

Lash, Joseph P. *Roosevelt and Churchill.* New York: W. W. Norton, 1976.

Lord, Walter. *Day of Infamy.* London: Longmans, Green, and Co., 1957.

Love, Robert W., Jr., ed. *Pearl Harbor Revisited.* New York: St. Martin's Press, 1995.

Kimmel, Husband E. *Admiral Kimmel's Story.* Chicago: Regnery, 1955.

Kimmett, Larry, and Margaret Regis. *The Attack on Pearl Harbor.* Seattle: Navigator, 1999.

Kinura, Yukiko. *Issei.* Honolulu: University of Hawaii Press, 1988.

Knaefler, Tomi Kaizawa. *Our House Divided.* Honolulu: University of Hawaii Press, 1991.

Lenihan, Daniel J. "The *Arizona* Revisited." *Natural History,* November 1991.

Meng, Chih. "Some Economic Aspects of the Sino-Japanese Conflict." *The Annals of the American Academy of Political and Social Science,* September 1938.

Nash, Vernon. "The Japanese-American War Myth." *The Nation,* December 11, 1935.

Oxford, Edward. "Prelude in the Pacific." *American History,* September/October 1991.

———. "One Sunday in December." *American History,* December 1998.

Prange, Gordon W. *At Dawn We Slept.* New York: Penguin Books, 1981.

———, with Donald M. Goldstein and Katherine V. Dillon. *December 7, 1941.* New York: McGraw-Hill, 1988.

———, with Donald M. Goldstein and Katherine V. Dillon. *God's Samurai.* Washington, D.C.: Brassey's, 1990.

Rancourt, Linda M. "Remembering Manzanar." *National Parks,* May/June 1993.

Rees, David. *The Defeat of Japan.* Westport, Conn.: Praeger, 1997.

Rodriggs, Lawrence Reginald. *We Remember Pearl Harbor.* Newark, California: Communications Concepts, 1991.

Slackman, Michael. *Target: Pearl Harbor.* Honolulu: University of Hawaii Press, 1990.

Smith, Carl. *Pearl Harbor.* Oxford: Osprey, 1999.

Stillwell, Paul, ed. *Air Raid: Pearl Harbor.* Annapolis, Md.: Naval Institute Press, 1981.

"Survivor's Remembrances." *Pearl Harbor Remembered.* October 16, 2000. <http://www.execpc.com/~ds chaaf/personal.html>

Taylor, A. J. P. *The Origins of the Second World War.* New York: Simon & Schuster, 1961.

Travers, Paul Joseph. *Eyewitness to Infamy.* Lanham, Md.: Madison Books, 1991.

Trefousse, Hans Louis, ed. *What Happened at Pearl Harbor?* New York: Wayne Publishers, 1958.

Tsukano, John. *Bridge of Love.* Honolulu: Hawaii Hosts, 1986.

Wisniewski, Richard A. *Pearl Harbor and the USS* Arizona *Memorial.* Honolulu: Pacific Basin Enterprises, 1986.

Young, Stephen Bower. *Trapped at Pearl Harbor.* Annapolis, Md.: Naval Institute Press, 1991.

Yu, C. John. "Joseph Yoshisuke Kurihara." *Disillusionment.* February 3, 1997. <http://www.oz.net/~cyu/inte rnment/kurihara.html>.

Wohlstetter, Roberta. *Pearl Harbor: Warning and Decision.* Stanford, Calif. Stanford University Press, 1962.

Zinsser, William. "At Pearl Harbor There Are New Ways to Remember." *Smithsonian,* December 1991.

Acknowledgments

I am indebted to the skillful staff of Tehabi Books and the expert reviewers who energetically assisted with this project. I am especially grateful for the research assistance of Susan Bischoff Mackin and Richard Kay and, most of all, for the encouragement and patience of my husband, David Hagerman, and our daughters, Emily and Casey.

—Susan Wels

San Francisco

Coming home

Elated Allied prisoners of war, *opposite,* cheer their release from a Japanese prisoner-of-war camp near Yokohama in August 1945.

Facing forward

Today, Pearl Harbor is a place of remembrance as well as a strategic center for U.S. military forces. Headquarters for the commander in chief of the United States Pacific Command, it is home to the U.S. Pacific Fleet, the Pacific air forces, the Pacific army forces, and the Pearl Harbor Naval Shipyard *(right)*.

Index

Greeting card

Lapel pin

Scrap book from the Pennsylvania

Sheet-music cover

Index continued

Match-book cover

War propaganda poster

WWII banner that signified a family casualty

Photo Credits

American Stock/Archive Photos: 216

AMMA/Douglas Peebles Photography: 23, 72b, 84 100c, 105, 111, 112, 123, 126, 130bc, 132, 135, 164b, 169ab, 170b, 176b, 178b, 184, 191b, 206a, 221a

Antonio Petruccilli Illustration/Rick Starkman Photography: 79a

AP/ Wide World Photo: 37, 46, 48–49, 54, 55

Archive Photos: 51, 53, 68, 177a

C. S. Bailey Illustrations: 6–7, 62–63, 151a–c, 210–211

Corbis Images/Bettman: 166, 168–169

Cory Lum/The Honolulu Adviser: 18

Digital Imagery © 2000 PhotoDisc, Inc.: 45, 52–53, 54–55, 59, 69, 78–79, 80–81, 98–99, 106–7, 138, 140, 166, 171, 177, 180, 188, 191, 196, 198, 212, 214

Dmitri Kessel/TimePix: 185

Douglas Peebles Photography: 4–5, 58, 82–83, 207ab, 218–219

***Fortune* © 1940 Time Inc. All rights reserved/Rick Starkman Photography:** 79b

Franklin D. Roosevelt Library, Hyde Park, New York: 42, 44, 47b, 56–57, 175, 177b, 196–197, 198

Frederic A. Reinecke Photography/The Authentic History Center: www.authentichistory.com: 187, 195b, 208, 220ab, 221b, 222b, 223

Gordon Jones Collection: 212

Gordon Jones/National Archives: (80–G–32837) 27, (80–G–32835) 212–213

Hawaii State Archives: 86–87, 91, 92–93, 191a

Jack Evans Collection: 89, 215a

John Bowles Collection: 214a–c

John Phillips/TimePix: 171

Library of Congress, Prints and Photographs Division: (LCMS–78663–1 222140) 155

National Archives: (18–0188) 16, (NSHS–21–DCH1–NIHC–HC298–298 R ExH.14 (6)5) 24–25, (242–HAP–1928–(46)) 32–33, (242–EB–7–38) 36b, (306–NT–2743V) 39, (179WP1035) 65a, (179WP1225) 65b, (179WP1297) 65c, (179WP1385) 179, (18–0958) 186–187, (28–1286) 190, (28–1171) 197 , (28–1486) 199 , (NLT–AVC–PHT–63(1457)29 200, (179WP454) 222a

National Park Service, USS *Arizona* Memorial/Tom Freeman Illustrations: 104–105, 110, 116–117, 124–125, 131, 139

Naval Historical Foundation: (NH 72273 KN) 1, (NH 50932) 8–9, (80 G 19948) 10–11, (80 G 32640) 13, (80 G 32463) 22, (NH 97378) 28–29, (208 CN 3992) 31, (NH 81942) 60, (NH 48589) 60, (NH 76462 KN) 66a, (NH 73060) 66b, (80–G–7919) 94, (NH 73062) 106, (80 G 71198) 112–13, (80 G 32836) 114, (NH 50473) 115, (80 G 19944) 118, (80 G 33035) 119, (NH 59030) 120–121, (80–G–32456) 122–123, (80–G–19942) 127, (80–G–40056) 128–129, (80–G–K–13513) 130a, (80–G–19941) 132–133, (USA C–5904) 136–137, (NH 58524) 140–141, (80–G–16871) 142–143, (80–G–32719) 144, (80–G–32896) 156–157, (NH 50926) 160–161, (80–G–32915) 164a, (19949) 170a, (NH 91331) 176a, (NH 63915) 180a, (NH 63916) 180b, (80–G–410534) 180c, (NH 64496) 180d, (83056) 180–181e, (80–G–64768) 180–181f, (NH 63919) 182, (NH–73064) 189, (NH 95582) 192–193, (NH 51382) 194a, (NH 63423) 194b, (NH–73065) 195a, (USAF 11462 A.C.) 202a, (80–G–490317) 202b, (USA C–2719) 203, (80–G–490313) 204–205, (USA C–4627) 206b, (80–G–K–13328) 209

Parada & Wedroch Collection: 33

Pat Thompson Collection: 100ab, 215b

Pat Thompson Collection/Rick Starkman Photography: 215c

Pictorial Histories Publishing Co.: 43

Rick Starkman Photography: 215d

San Diego Aerospace Museum: 45ab, 101, 138, 162

The Mainichi Newspapers: 50, 74–75, 200–201, 201

Thomas McAvoy/TimePix: 67, 70–71, 156, 158, 159, 165, 167

U.S. Senator Daniel K. Inouye Archives: 17, 19

USS *Arizona* Memorial, National Park Service: 2–3, 14–15, 20–21, 26, 30, 61, 64, 69, 72a, 73, 76, 77, 78, 78–79, 80, 81ab, 85, 88, 90, 95, 96–97, 99, 102–103, 108–9, 134–135, 141, 152–153, 154, 163, 172–173, 174, 178a, 213

United States Holocaust Memorial Museum: 34–35, 36a, 38, 40–41, 47a

William Shrout/TimePix: 71

continued from front

December 7, 1941

Thomas Larcy Kirkpatrick • Edward Klann • William August Klasing • Otto C. Klein • Chester Fredrick Kleist • Robert Edwin Kline • Francis Lawrence Klopp • Roderick Otto Klubertanz • Milto
Jewel Knight Jr. • Robert Wagner Knight • Verne Francis Knipp • William Knubel Jr. • Walter Ernest Koch • Clarence D. Koenekamp • Herman Oliver Koeppe • John J. Kohl • Brosig Kolajajc
• Edward Koichi Kondo • Albert Joseph Konnick • John Anthony Kosec • Robert Kovar • Leonard Joseph Kozelek • James Albert Krahn • Donald J. Kraker • James Henry Kramb • John Davi
Kramb • Harry Wellington Kramer • Robert Rudolph Kramer • Fred Joseph Krause • Max Sam Krissman • Richard Warren Kruger • Adolph Louis Kruppa • William Paul Kubinec • Conra
Kujawa • Howard Helgi Kukuk • Stanley Kula • Donald Joseph Kusie • Ernest George Kuzee • Hans C. Kvalnes • William Lester Kvidera • D. T. Kyser • William Richard La France • Ralph
La Mar • George Willard La Rue • Willard Dale La Salle • Daniel La Verne • Henry E. Lacrosse Jr. • Robert Paul Laderach • John Ervin Lake Jr. • Donald Lapier Lakin • Joseph Jordan Laki
• George Samuel Lamb • Kenneth Taft Lamons • John Thomas Lancaster • Henry Landman • James Joseph Landry Jr. • Edward Wallace Lane • Mancel Curtis Lane • Richard Charles Lang
• Orville J. Langenwalter • Frank J. Lango • Henry John Lanouette • Donald C. V. Larsen • Elliott Deen Larsen • Leonard Carl Larson • Bleecker Lattin • Johnnie Cornelius Laurie • Charle
Lawrence • Edward Stephen Lawrence • Elmer Patterson Lawrence • Willard Irvin Lawson • Thomas Francis Leary • Carroll Volney Lee Jr. • Henry Lloyd Lee • Isaac William Lee • Ro
Elmer Lee Jr. • David Alonzo Leedy • John Goldie Leggett • Joseph McNeil Legros • Gerald George Lehman • Myron Kenneth Lehman • Malcolm Hedrick Leigh • James Webster Leight • Josep
Sam L. Lemire • Robert Lawrence Leopold • Edmond Brayton Lepper • Lionel W. Lescault • George G. Leslie • Steve Louie Lesmeister • Frank Levar • Sherman Levine • James I. Lewis
John Earl Lewis • Theodore J. Lewis • Wayne Alman Lewis • Neil Stanley Lewison • Lester H. Libolt • Worth Ross Lightfoot • Gordon Ellsworth Linbo • John William Lincoln • James E. Lindsa
• James Mitchell Lindsay • Harold William Lindsey • John Herbert Lindsley • George Edward Linton • Wilbur Thomas Lipe • Clarence William Lipke • John Anthony Lipple • Daniel Edwar
Lisenby • Eugene Victor Lish • John Grubbs III Little • Raymond Edward Livers • Wayne Nicholas Livers • Alfred Eugene Livingston • Richard E. Livingston • Douglas A. Lock • Clarence M
Lockwood • Adolph John Loebach • Earl Wynne Lohman • Frank Stuart Lomax • Marciano Lomibao • James Edward London • Benjamin Franklin Long • Guy Edward Long • Tai Chung Lo
• Peter Souza Lopes • Harry W. Lord Jr. • Thomas William Lounsbury • Charles Bernard Loustanau • Carl Robert Love • Frank Crook Loveland • William Joseph Lovshin • Robert S. Lowe
Neil Jermiah Lucey • Vernon Thomas Luke • Royle Bradford Luker • James Edward Luna • Jack Leon Lunsford • John Kallervo Luntta • Howard N. Lusk • William Edward Lutschan Jr.
Ernest Burton Luzier • Donald William Lynch • Emmett Isaac Lynch • James Robert Lynch Jr. • Kenneth Lee Lynch • William Joseph Lynch Jr. • Arnold Eugene Lyon • Lawrence P. Lyons Jr.
Octavius Mabine • Thomas Samuel Macy • Raymond Dudley Maddox • Arthur John Madrid • Andres Franquez Mafnas • Francisco Reyes Mafnas • Gerald James Magee • Howard Scott Mager
• Joseph Malatak • Frank Edward Malecki • Michael Malek • Algeo Victor Malfante • John Stanley Malinowski • Harry Lynn Malson • George Jay Manganelli • Howard Ellis Manges • Edwar
Paul Manion • William Manley • Arthur Cleon Manlove • Charles Willis Mann • John H. Mann • William Edward Mann • Leroy Manning • Milburn Alex Manning • Walter Benjamin Mannin
• Robert Francis Manske • Steve Matt Marinich • Elwood Henry Maris • Robert Harold Markley • Joseph Henry Marling • Urban Herschel Marlow • Benjamin Raymond Marsh Jr. • Willia
Arthur Marsh • John Andrew Marshall • Thomas Donald Marshall • William Earl Marshall Jr. • Dale Lewis Martin • George M. Martin Jr • Herbert Benjamin Martin • Hugh Lee Martin
James Albert Martin • James Orrwell Martin • John Winter Martin • Luster Lee Martin • Wallace R. Martin • Rudolph Machado Martinez • Andrew Michael Marze • Byron Dalley Mason
Henri Clay Mason • James Edward Massey • Clyde Harold Mastel • Dayton Monroe Masters • Cleburne E. Carl Masterson • Maurice Mastrototaro • Jesus Manalisay Mata • Harold Richar
Mathein • Charles Harris Mathison • Donald Joseph Mathison • Vernon Merferd Matney • Harell K. Mattox • James Durant Mattox • Joseph Keith Maule • Louis Eugene May • George Frederic
Maybee • Frazier Mayfield • Lester Ellsworth Mayfield • Marvin William Mayo • Rex Haywood Mayo • William E. McAbee • John Scott McAllen • Luther Kirk McBee • Edwin Bonner McCab
• Joseph McCabe Sr. • James Francis McCarrens •William Moore McCary • John Charles McClafferty • Thomas Alfred McClelland • James Jacob McClintock • Donald Robert McCloud • Harve
Manford McClung • Lawrence Jennings McCollom • Clarence William McComas • Warren Harrell McCutcheon • James Oliver McDonald • Lawrence James McFaddin • Lester Fred McGhee
Joe Otis McGlasson • Samme Willie Genes McGrady • George V. McGraw • Edward L. McGuckin • Francis Raymond McGuire • John Breckenridge McHughes • Dencil Jeoffrey McIntosh • Har
George McIntosh • Quentin Guy McKee • Bert Eugene McKeenan • Russell McKinnie • Hale McKissack • Michael Martin McKosky • Herbert McLaughlin • Lloyd Elden McLaughlin • Stanley
McLeod • Clyde Clifton McMeans • Aaron L. McMurtrey • John Blair McPherson • Robert Cameron McQuade • Durward A. Meadows • Donald F. Meagher • Louis Means • John Morga
Meares • Joseph Alford Medlen • John Anthony Meglis • Earl Rudolph Melton • Herbert Franklin Melton • John Russell Melton • Enrique Castro Mendiola • James Austin Menefee • Herbe
Hugo Menges • Vicente Gogue Meno • Stanley Paul Menzenski • William W. Merithew • Howard Deal Merrill • Horace Arthur Messam • Victor L. Meyers • Charles O. Michael • Carlo Anthor
Micheletto • John Franklin Middleswart • Torao Migita • Jesse Keith Milbourne • Archie Theodore Miles • Oscar Wright Miles • Chester John Miller • Doyle Allen Miller • Forrest Newton Mill
• George Stanley Miller • J. B. Delane Miller • Jessie Zimmer Miller • John David Miller • Marvin Eugene Miller • William Cicero Miller • William Oscar Miller • Weldon Harvey Milligan
James William Milner • Robert Lang Mims • Richard J. Minear Jr. • Orville Ray Minix • James Dewey Minter • Bernard Joseph Mirello • Joe Eddie Mister • Edwin N. Mitchell • John G. Mitche
• Wallace Gregory Mitchell • Joseph Mlinar • Richard Preston Molpus • Donald Monroe • Charles Andrew Montgomery • Robert E. Montgomery • Wallace Alford Montgomery • William
Montgomery • Robert Edward Moody • Clyde Carson Moore • Douglas Carlton Moore • Fred Kenneth Moore • James Carlton Moore • Lionel Jay Moorhead • William Starks Moorhouse
Russell Lee Moorman • George A. Moran • Wayne Morgan • James Orries Morgareidge • Edo Morincelli • Eugene Elvis Morley • Elmer R. Morrell • Emmett Edloe Morris • Owen Newto
Morris • William Francis Morris • Earl Leroy Morrison • Edward Francis Morrissey • Edward Charles Morse • Francis Jerome Morse • George Robert Morse • Norman Roi Morse • Joseph
Moser • Louis Gustav Moslener Jr. • Tommy Lee Moss • Francis Clayton Mostek • Gordon Eddy Moulton • Albin John Mrace • Joseph Alexander Muhofski • John Mark Mulick • Claude Mun
• Charles Luther Murdock • Melvin Elijah Murdock • James Joseph Murphy • James Palmer Murphy • Jessie Huell Murphy • Thomas J. Murphy Jr. • Clair Clifton Myers • James Gernie Mye
• Ray Harrison Myers • Erwin H. Naasz • Alexander Joseph Nadel • George Eugene Naegle • Hugh Kenneth Naff • Masayoshi Nagamine • Elmer Denton Nail • Paul Andrews Nash • Jam
Garland Nations • Morris Edward Nations • J D Naylor • Tom Dick Neal • Charles Raymond Necessary • La Verne J. Needham • Don Ocle Neher • Paul Neipp • Joseph F. Nelles • Geor
Nelsen • Harl Coplin Nelson • Henry Clarence Nelson • Lawrence Adolphus Nelson • Marlyn Wayne Nelson • Richard Eugene Nelson • Earl Tilman Nermoe • William F. Neuendorf Jr. • Arthur
Neuenschwander • Sam Douglas Nevill • Laxton Gail Newman • Paul Eugene Newton • Wayne Edward Newton • Wilbur Francis Newton • Alfred Rose Nichols • Bethel Allan Nichols • Ca
Nichols • Clifford Leroy Nichols • Harry Ernest Nichols • Louis Duffie Nichols • Glen Eldon Nicholson • Hancel Grant Nicholson • Frank Edward Nicoles • Thomas James Nides • Arnold Mads
Nielsen • Floyd Theadore Nielsen • Laverne Alious Nigg • Joe Raymond Nightingale • Charles Edward Nix • Emile Salvatore Noce • Henry Ellis Nolatubby • Robert Harold Noonan

In Memoriam

onald Charles Norman • Orris Nate Norman • William M. Northway • Alwyn Berry Norvelle • Theodore Lucian Nowosacki • Raymond Alfred Nusser • Frank Erskine Nye • Joseph Bernard 'Brien • George David O'Bryan • Joseph Benjamin O'Bryan • Henry Francis Ochoski • Maurice Michael O'Connor • Yaeko Lillian Oda • Edwin Nelson Odgaard • Virgil Simon Off • William H. ffutt • Charles Ralph Ogle • Victor Willard Ogle • Lonnie Harris Oglesby • Camillus M. O'Grady • Frank Ohashi • Hayako Ohta • Janet Yumiko Ohta • Kiyoko Ohta • Clifford Nathan Olds • aymond Brown Oliver • Edward Kern Olsen • Eli Olsen • Glen Martin Olson • Rex Eugene O'Neall • William Thomas O'Neill Jr. • Barbara June Ornellas • Gertrude Ornellas • Dwight Jerome rr • Willard C. Orr • Dean Baker Orwick • Stanislaus Joseph Orzech • Mervin Eugene Osborne • Leland Grimstead Ostrander • Peter Dean Ott • Carl William Otterstetter • Jarvis Godwin utland • Lawrence Jack Overley • Fredrick Halden Owen • James Patrick Owens • Richard Allen Owens • Alphard Stanley Owsley • Arnold Jacob Owsley • Thomas Lea Owsley • Amos Paul ace • Joseph Wilson Pace • Millard Clarence Pace • Walter Joseph Paciga • James Palides Jr. • Calvin Harry Palmer • Wilferd Dewey Palmer • Harry Tuck Lee Pang • James Alfred Paolucci George Lawrence Paradis • Elmer Anthony Parker • Isaac Parker • June Winton Parker • Harry Edward Parkes • Chester Lloyd Parks • Peter John Paroli • Clarence Rankin Patterson • lmer Marvin Patterson • Harold Lemuel Patterson • Richard Patterson Jr. • Hilery Paulmand • Bruno Pavini • Raymond Paul Pawlowski • Kenneth Morris Payne • Robert Hopkins Peak • lonzo Pearce Jr. • Dale Ferrell Pearce • Norman Cecil Pearson • Robert Stanley Pearson • William Howard Peavey • Eugene Edward Peck • Howard William Peckham • Francis James Pedrotti Max Valdyne Peery • Michael Peleschak • John Arthur Peltier • John Wallace Pence • George E. Pendarvis • Raymond Pennington • Russell M. Penny • John Campbell Pensyl • Walter Ray entico • Howard Lee Penton • George Ames Penuel Jr. • Stephen Pepe • Charles Fred Perdue • George Ernest Perkins • Forrest Hurbert Perry • Hal H. Perry Jr. • Albert H. Peterson Jr. • Elroy ernon Peterson • Hardy Wilbur Peterson • Roscoe Earl Peterson • Charles Ross Pettit • Wiley James Petway • John Joseph Petyak • Robert Albert Petz • George Edward Phelps • James ichard Philbin • Thomas F. Philipsky • James William Phillips • Milo Elah Phillips • James Norman Phipps • Alexander Louis Piasecki • Sidney Pierce • Jay E. Pietzsch • Harvey Lee Pike • ewis Jackson Pike • Albert Wesley Pinkham • Andrew Anthony Pinko • Gerald Homer Pirtle • Rudolph Victor Piskuran • Jack Arthur Pitcher • Walter Giles Pitcher • Lewis William Pitts Jr. • onald D. Plant • Daniel P. Platschorre • Herbert J. Poindexter Jr. • Walter Howard Ponder • Elmer Leo Pool • Ralph Ernest Poole • Robert Kirk Porterfield • Damian Maraya Portillo • Frank S. E. osey • Darrell Albert Post • George Povesko • Jack Speed Powell • Raymond E. Powell • Thomas George Powell • William J. Powell • Abner Franklin Power • Joe O'Neil Powers • Roy Wallace owers • Daniel J. Powloski • Wayne Harold Presson • Brady Oliver Prewitt • Robert Lamb Pribble • Arland Earl Price • George Price • George Franklin Price • John A. Price • Lewis Bailey ride Jr. • Robert Leo Pritchett Jr. • Alexsander J. Przybysz • Edwin Lester Puckett • Jasper Langley Pue Jr. • John Pugh Jr. • Roy Alfred Pullen • Nolan Eugene Pummill • Avis Boyd Putnam Edward Puzio • Mike Joseph Quarto • Jose Sanchez Quinata • Edward Joseph Quirk • Edward Stanley Racisz • Neal Jason Radford • Allen G. Rae • Paul Smith Raimond • John Thomas ainbolt • Richard Redner Rall • Arthur Severin Rasmussen • Warren D. Rasmussen • George Vernon Rasmusson • William Ratkovich • Glen Donald Rawhouser • Clyde Jackson Rawson • ldon Casper Ray • Harry Joseph Ray • Dan Edward Reagan • Casbie Reaves • Clay Cooper Rector • John Jeffris Reece • Frank Edward Reed • James Buchanan Reed Jr. • Ray Ellison Reed Thomas J. Reeves • Leo Basil Regan • Paul James Register • George Beard Reid • William Henry Reid • Rudolph Herbert Reinhold • Albert Renner • Jack Martin Restivo • Herman C. Reuss Earl Arthur Reynolds • Jack Franklyn Reynolds • Birb Richard Rhodes • Mark Alexander Rhodes • William T. Rhodes • Irvin Franklin Rice • William Albert Rice • William Hurst Rice • ilson Albert Rice • Claude Edward Rich • Porter Leigh Rich • Raymond Lyle Richar • Warren John Richardson • Joseph L. Richey • Robert M. Richey • Fred Louis Richison • Albert Wallace ichter • Leonard Claiver Richter • Guadalupe Augustine Rico • Eugene Edward Riddell • Clyde Ridenour Jr. • Fred Riganti • Gerald Herald Riggins • David Joseph Riley • Edwin Herbert ipley • Francisco Unpingoo Rivera • Russell Clyde Roach • Anson E. Robbins • Dwight Fisk Roberts • Earl Reed Roberts • Kenneth Franklin Roberts • McClellan Taylor Roberts • Walter Scott oberts Jr. • Wilburn Carle Roberts • William Francis Roberts • Edgar Robertson Jr. • James Milton Robertson • Joseph Morris Robertson • Harold Thomas Robinson • James Henry Robinson James William Robinson • John James Robinson • Robert Warren Robinson • Mark Clifton Robison • Raymond Arthur Roby • John Dayton Rodgers • Eugene Oscar Roe • Harry Turner oehm • Harold William Roesch • Thomas Sprugeon Rogers • Walter Boone Rogers • Halvor E. Rogness • Simon Romano • Donald Roger Rombalski • Vladimir M. Romero • Emil Oliver onning • Melvin Lenord Root • Chester Clay Rose • Ernest Claude Rose • Howard Arthur Rosenau • Orval Albert Rosenbery • Alfred Aaron Rosenthal • Deane Lundy Ross • Joe Boyce Ross William Fraser Ross • Joseph Carel Rouse • Eugene Joseph Rowe • Frank Malcom Rowell • William Nicholas Royals • Howard Dale Royer • Frank Willard Royse • John Frank Rozar • seph Stanley Rozmus • Cecil Roy Ruddock • William Ruggerio • Robert Gleason Runckel • Nicholas Runiak • Charles Lee Ruse • Richard Perry Rush • Orville Lester Rusher • Harvey George ıshford • Joseph John Ruskey • Benjamin Nelson Russell • Arthur William Russett • John Peter Rutkowski • Dale Andrew Ruttan • Edmund Thomas Ryan • Roman Walter Sadlowski • Morris anklin Saffell • Glenn Dawain Sahl • Kenneth Harlan Sampson • Sherley Rolland Sampson • Merrill Keith Sandall • Dean Stanley Sanders • Eugene Thomas Sanders • James Harvey anderson • Thomas Steger Sanford • Filomeno Santos • William Ford Sather • Theodore Hilliard Saulsbury • Charles Louis Saunders • Lyal Jackson Savage • Walter Samuel Savage Jr. • hn Edwin Savidge • Tom Savin • Michael Savinski • Paul Edd Saylor • Joseph Schdowski • George Albert Scheuerlein • William Rhinehart Schick • Ernest Schiller • Benjamin Schlect • uis Schleifer • Walter Fay Schleiter • Elmer Pershing Schlund • George R. Schmersahl • Herman Schmidt • Vernon Joseph Schmidt • Aloysius Herman Schmitt • Andrew James Schmitz • illiam Jacob Schneider • John Harry Schoonover • Robert L. Schott • Harold Arthur Schrank • Henry Schroeder • Herman Lincoln Schuman • Richard Martin Schuon Jr. • John Schurr • erbert C. Schwarting • Harold Hugh Scilley • A. J. Scott • Bernard Oliver Scott • Crawford Edward Scott • George Harrison Scott • George William Scott • Ralph Edward Scott • Robert aymond Scott • Jack Leo Scruggs • Russell Otto Seaman • Erwin Leroy Searle • Chester Ernest Seaton • Verdi Delmore Sederstrom • William Eugene Seeley • William Lawrence Sellon • erett Iven Severinson • Charles Clifton Sevier • William Kenneth Shafer • William James Shanahan Jr. • William Alfred Shannon • Harry Robert Sharbaugh • Lewis Purdie Sharon • Robert R. attuck • Donald Robert Shaum • Clyde Donald Shaw • Robert K. Shaw • George Robert Sheffer • Edward Judson Shelden • Russell K. Shelly Jr. • Robert O. Sherman • Warren Joseph errill • Richard Stanton Sherven • William F. Shields • Harold Ely Shiffman • Paul Eugene Shiley • Melvin Irvin Shimer • Gordon Eshom Shive • Malcolm Holman Shive • Benjamin Franklin ively • Shelby Charles Shook • Irland Shores Jr. • Henson Taylor Shouse • Marvin John Shugart • Delmar Dale Sibley • Russell Lewis Sidders • John Henry Sidell • William Garfield Silva William Howard Silva • Jesse Silvey • Carleton Elliott Simensen • Frank Leroy Simmons • Tceollyar Simmons • Walter Hamilton Simon • Albert Eugene Simpson • Eugene Mitchell Skaggs Harvey Leroy Skeen • Charley Jackson Skiles Jr. • Eugene Skiles • Garold Leroy Skiles • Edward Frank Slapikas • Earl Clifton Sletto • Martin Rueben Slifer • Jack G. Smalley • George vid Smart • Joseph Gillespie Smartt • Halge Hojem Smestad • Albert Joseph Smith • Earl Smith Jr. • Earl Walter Smith • Edward Smith • George J. Smith • George Randolph Smith • Gerald ven Smith • Gordon Ellsworth Smith • Harry Smith • Harry E. Smith • John A. Smith • John Edward Smith • Keith Vodden Smith • Leonard Ferdnay Smith • Lloyd George Smith •